It's never the wrong time to meet ordinary people living in an extraordinary place and to be reminded of all that is good, at times even holy, in that place. That's exactly what Bret Lott does in *Gather the Olives*, a memoir of his experiences in Israel of people, places, and food, told in an engaging voice by turns wondrous, charming, tender, humorous and, as are the people we meet along the way, fully, deeply human.

—**Richard Chess**, author of *Love Nailed to the Doorpost*

How to respond to a book about Israel published in a time of war and division that is not about terrorists, genocide, rape, hostages, bombs, and failed leadership? As a Jew who spends an inordinate amount of each day consumed with the daily tragedies, I approached warily. This is what I found: Bret Lott has written a book of heart, and kindness, with gorgeous prose that reminds us of the beauty of the land, and the value of life. He eschews stereotypes, celebrates humanity and, without sentimentality, gives us hope for the future. This is the travelogue that I would recommend to any of my friends heading to—or thinking about—that part of the world. Even now. Especially now.

—**Richard Michelson**, National Jewish Book Award Winner

Olives, yes, but *za'atar* and cherries, earthy cheeses, lemon-mint water, and so many more gifts from friends and strangers are gathered here at this most capacious table. Bret Lott writes with the eye of a Dutch Master, the soul of a poet, and a heart that loves people in all their unconventional beauty and prickly complexity. Every daily walk, chance meeting, close call, and shared meal is sensually observed, wide open to wonder, and tuned to the ways hope might be found in the most fragile, yet soul-sustaining moments.

—**Lia Purpura**, author of *All the Fierce Tethers*

In *Gather the Olives*, his memoir of his years in the Holy Land, Bret Lott does what seems almost impossible to do. He offers us taste after taste of the food—gift after gift—he was invited to share with friends over the years: the Shabat feasts, fresh fruit—especially those cherries--and vegetables and wine (including even *treif* bacon and ribs at times). But he offers other tastes as well: the landscapes of Nazareth and Bethlehem and Jerusalem, but also Petra and the Golan Heights from the summit. And—most importantly—he gives us the taste of real friendship, and the extraordinary generosity of those Israeli doctors along the Syrian borders caring for Syrian soldiers and mothers and children. As he himself so eloquently phrases it, "Somehow, in this tablespoonful of green and bitter herbs mixed with other spices and seeds, I am partaking of the history of my faith, tasting time and place and salvation." This book is a must read.

—**Paul Mariani**, University Professor of English emeritus, Boston College

To behold *Gather the Olives* is to admire Bret Lott as a painter of words growing out of the Holy soil. Bret's stories cultivate the fecund, but fractured, earth of generational memories, to remind us of what writing can do, and of what writing can become. Every word is to be savored in this poignant American memoir excavated in Israel, a conflicted land of surprising encounters, of indelible generosity, and of miraculous abundance.

—**Makoto Fujimura**, artist and author of *Art+Faith: A Theology of Making*

Gather
the
Olives

Books by Bret Lott

The Man Who Owned Vermont
A Stranger's House
A Dream of Old Leaves
Jewel
Reed's Beach
Fathers, Sons and Brothers
How to Get Home
The Hunt Club
A Song I Knew by Heart
The Difference Between Women and Men
Before We Get Started
Ancient Highway
Dead Low Tide
Letters and Life

BRET LOTT

Gather
the
Olives

On Food and Hope and the Holy Land

SL/NT
BOOKS

Slant Books
P.O. Box 60295
Seattle, WA 98160

www.slantbooks.org

Cataloguing-in-Publication data:

Names: Lott, Bret

Title: Gather the olives: on food and hope and the holy land / Bret Lott

Description: Seattle, WA: Slant Books, 2024

Identifiers: ISBN 978-1-63982-163-1 (hardcover) | ISBN 978-1-63982-162-4 (paperback) | ISBN 978-1-63982-164-8 (ebook)

Subjects: LCSH: Cooking, Mediterranean | Food--Israel | Food habits--Israel | Israel--Description and travel

For Melanie, as ever and always

For he satisfies the longing soul,
　　and the hungry soul he fills with good things.

Psalm 107:9

They will come and shout for joy on the heights of Zion;
　　they will rejoice in the bounty of the Lord—
the grain, the new wine and the olive oil,
　　the young of the flocks and herds.
They will be like a well-watered garden
　　and they will sorrow no more.

Jeremiah 31:12

We must eat.

M. F. K. Fisher

Contents

A Word

I TURNED THIS BOOK IN to the publisher in the summer of 2023. Then came the horrors of October 7th and after.

Immediately these pages became missives from Before, and now, as you read these words, they are operating in the After.

There is no going back.

Yet here is a book. It is about food, and about communion. It is about taste, and about people, and place. It is about breaking bread, and with whom we break it. My wife, Melanie, and I lived in Jerusalem for a while—five months, to be exact—and have stayed there for extended periods for, at last count, a half dozen times. We have traveled to the West Bank, to East Jerusalem, and to Ramallah. We have been to one side and the other of the wall, and found good and beautiful people on both. But let it be known that I am no expert on Israel, no professional guide or apologist or even dilettante. Please don't imagine this will be anything like a cookbook or a list of suggested tours.

Or a book on war, barbarity, retribution or responses measured or disproportionate. It is not a book on social justice, or political stance, or a solving of the Middle East situation, one state or two state or war or peace protracted or paused. By the time you read these words, the world will have moved forward into realms unknown, and even these terms I've paraded about just now will seem antiquated because of whatever new news will have arrived via the predictable ways news of the world arrives.

This is a book about another story to this place. One of people to people, and the way, when sharing a meal, whether cherries from a roadside stand or pork ribs sauced and grilled on the stoop of an Arabic apartment, there can be peace.

We lived there, and visited, and have partaken in meals with more people through the years, Israeli and Palestinian alike, than we can count, from falafel with newfound friends at the best street-corner shawarma stand in Jerusalem's German Colony, the place set with maybe a dozen plastic chairs and a window out onto the street; to a lunch of innumerable fresh salads cluttered across a flowered plastic tablecloth in a family's home at the border with Lebanon, the father seeking to restore the Aramaic language as far and wide as he can; to a food truck hamburger at a minor-league baseball game, the diamond settled in a field of sunflowers outside Beit-Shemesh, where the ark of the covenant first came to rest after the Philistines had sent the tumor-inducing thing back to Israel on a wooden cart pulled by those straight-arrow milch cows.

We've eaten in a lot of places. And we have met good people all along the way.

This is a book about them. This is a book about their places. This is a book about their food. It is an account from Before, yes, but it is an account of the way food and place and people inform and enlighten and broaden and magnify what it means to be human.

Now that we are After, there is no going back.

But now, as forever, there is hope.

With this book, I am trying to give a glimpse of that hope. Because hope still lives.

First Morning

I'M THE ONLY one here, and I'm hungry.

Early morning, the restaurant bright with sunlight in through the huge glass wall to the right, the other walls all calm and stoic limestone, like the rest of everything here at Mishkenot Sha'ananim. It's a guest house, though more a small private hotel than anything else, for artists and authors, musicians and thinkers staying in the city for one reason and another. The limestone walls of the hotel's single hallway—there are only a couple dozen rooms—are lined with photos of past visitors: Pablo Casals, Saul Bellow, Grace Paley, Isaac Stern, the Dalai Lama, and more.

Somehow, they let me in the place.

And this is its restaurant. Maybe twenty tables in four rows before me, each set with a crisp white tablecloth, a small vase of fresh flowers at its center. Nobody else here, save for a man in a white shirt and black pants, his back to me. He's standing at the bar/coffee station at the end of the glass wall, and he turns, the echo of my steps on the tile floor as I approach what has given me away.

He's a little older, short graying hair, shirtsleeves turned up once at the cuffs. He steps toward me, dips his head, smiles, then gestures to the empty tables with a slow sweep of his arm, a silent gameshow host introducing what might be won.

"Shalom," he finally says, the word almost a whisper for the quiet of an empty restaurant early in the morning.

"Shalom," I say, the word a little too loud out of me, and I nod. He turns, leads me into the rows, still with his hand sweeping around, and he says more words, ones I don't understand but that I know mean: The place is yours. Take any seat you want.

I've been awake all night, the flight from Prague arriving at 4:30 in Tel Aviv this morning. I'm tired. But I am happy, and hungry, and there's a quiet course of adrenalin in me. Because I am here.

I am in Israel. I am in Jerusalem. The place of all places.

And this is when I pause to look out that huge glass wall at the view. I've already seen it from the covered porch off my room here after I'd checked in, dropped my bags, taken a shower.

But it's a view I need to see again to try and make myself believe I am really here. I am really here:

The walls of the old city itself, maybe three hundred yards away and to the left across a low rocky valley. Crenellated limestone walls still in shadow for the rising sun behind them, the walls white but streaked with age. To the right of them stand more limestone buildings—a white belltower, a blue cone roof on another white building, white buildings in a kind of cascade down the forested sides of the promontory just over there, just over there: Mount Zion itself.

That's it, all right there. Those limestone walls, that hill with its white stone buildings. Old Jerusalem, and Mt. Zion.

The man says more words to me, all of them still just as quiet, and I turn from the window to him, see him paused at a table. As quietly as I can so as not to break the spell of any of this—the light, this place, the cool empty of the early morning—I say, "I don't speak Hebrew."

Our eyes meet for the first time, and he smiles, nods again, looks down at the table. "Is okay," he says, then, "How about here?" each word given a small space before the next, and he gives another nod, this time at the table, the matter decided.

He sets the table with a napkin and utensils I only now notice he has had in his hand the whole time, pulls out a chair, and says, "Coffee?"

"Yes, please," I say, then add "Bevakasha," one of the three or four words I've practiced before getting here: Please.

He looks up from the chair and smiles just a little wider now, his shoulders up only an instant and in the smallest way. "You speak Hebrew," he says, and sweeps his hand to the chair for me to sit.

And now I see past him, beyond the row of tables behind him, the breakfast buffet. Wedges of cheese, shiny stainless steel bowls of fruit, baskets of pastries, more bowls and more, all lit up as though for a play, arranged just so, with white tablecloths and shiny serving spoons and two stacks of plates to the left of it all.

Only what appears, at first glance, a breakfast buffet in a very nice hotel.

So, this is where we begin: first morning and first meal in Jerusalem.

Once I'm seated, once the coffee has arrived—an espresso, actually, in its little cup with its saucer and little spoon, to which I nod to the waiter and say "Toda" to impress him with the fact I also know Thank you in Hebrew—and after he has asked if I would like orange juice too—"Yes," I say, then, "Ken": word number four—and after I take a sip of the wonderfully bitter coffee after this very long and sleepless night, then drink the whole thing in two more sips, and after I marvel yet again at the view from this table of those walls, and Mt. Zion, it is time to go to the breakfast buffet, because I am hungry.

The three tables all in a row are a still life, everything perfect. Track lighting above gives the bowls and baskets and trays all a kind of dramatic presence, and because I am the first one here, I'm afraid of wrecking it all by digging in with one of those shiny serving spoons or hacking away with a cheese knife. So I stand for a few moments, surveying it all.

Watermelon, the deep matte red of all these cubes, beside it a bowl of pale orange cantaloupe, these in cubes too, and then cubes of cool green honeydew, and pineapple, and then orange wedges and grapefruit halves. Green grapes and red grapes. Apple slices miraculously white.

And here is a bowl of dates—dates, for breakfast!—shiny and the color of teak, their skins slightly puckered. More bowls: Kalamata olives in one, deep red and glistening with oil, green olives and herbs in another, black wrinkled olives in yet another. And more bowls, one with diced vegetables—tomatoes, red peppers, cucumbers, scallions—beside one with pale pink tuna salad in a nest of lettuce leaves beside a bowl of what may very well be tabbouleh for the tight mince of green, then roasted eggplant in a marinade, each shriveled round layered into the next to make a wheel of brown and purple and green.

All these vegetables for breakfast. And tuna fish too.

Cheeses then: white and yellow and orange wedges, a small wheel crusted in what may be ash, another in peppercorns, another wheel chalky white with sprigs of herbs on top. Typical fare, I'm thinking, but still a marvel of color and arrangement, and now here's a bowl of hardboiled eggs, and a basket of croissants and sliced bread and small iced buns—but rugelach in there too, and some sort of triangle- and square-shaped puff pastries, golden brown and, it would seem, filled with something—and now another basket with bagels, plain and sesame and salt and Everything, and a stack of halved pita the color of wheat.

Now four or five shallow bowls of cream cheeses, soft or slightly crumbly, chived or with bits of vegetables mixed in, and of course plain, perfect white. There's a wooden board with the thinnest slices of lox, bright pink trimmed with dill, beside it a row of ramekins filled with capers and slivers of red onions and chopped tomatoes. Next to them a bowl of what looks like yogurt but with herbs stirred in, a pool of green olive oil settled at its center, and then, at the end, a bowl of hummus, taupe with a sprinkle of pine nuts and some sort of green spice that seems to have sesame seeds in it, all of it drizzled with olive oil too.

I take a plate from the stack back at the beginning, spoon up some of those red cubes of watermelon, then two hardboiled eggs, a pita, and last, though I am even more afraid of breaking this spell than when I first stood and took all this in, I dig into the hummus, making certain to catch some of that oil, a touch of that green spice with its sesame seeds, and of course those pine nuts.

Why do I remember this all? Why is it, nearly twenty years after this arrival in the Holy Land, I recall the set of bowls, the light, the pool of green olive oil in that herbed yogurt, those puff pastries, the stack of pita for which, just now, I have searched for an hour to find the right word for their color in my memory, the word *wheat* only a dull imitation of what I remember as a stack of perfect pita, ready and ready?

Laban will be the name of that herbed yogurt-looking dish, I'll one day discover, and in my discovering discover too that everyone knows this—How could you not know this is *laban*? You've never heard of *laban*? Further confusing the matter will be that in some places the dish will be called *labneh*, that variation in names a partner to the fact the English spelling of words in Israel is something of a crapshoot, street names and buildings and towns on maps and in person oftentimes two or three different things. And yet that mix of cucumbers and peppers and scallions and tomatoes will be called, unwaveringly, Israeli Salad, and will appear at pretty much every meal we'll ever have in this country.

One day more than a year from this buffet, the mystery of how to tell what's in those shaped puff pastries will be revealed in a cafeteria at Bar-Ilan University in Tel Aviv where I will be teaching, a gang of my grad students marshalling me through the food stations for lunch my first day there. When we come to the pastry station, and when I remark that I love *burekas* (get this: they're sometimes spelled *bourekas*, but also *borekas* too), but that I can never figure out whether I'm going to get one filled with cheese or potato, the whole group freezes, looks at me opened-mouthed, agog at my naivete. Then one of them—a young man from Toronto who will years from then become an attorney back in Canada—will pull me by the elbow right up to the glass behind which sit the rows of baked goods, and tell me, "Triangles are cheese, squares are potato and, well, other things, but never cheese," and suddenly all will be made clear, the mystery solved.

One of those cream cheeses in the array of them over there—a pure white one but with a texture a little firmer, a touch crumbly—I will one day discover is called Bulgarian cream cheese, and will become my everlasting favorite for the bright lemony bite to it, its presence schmeared on a nice polite sesame bagel the perfect combination.

But none of this is available to me at this moment, here in an empty restaurant, my plate filled with those cubes of watermelon, those two eggs, a pita, and hummus.

I know hummus. I know watermelon, and eggs, and pita the color of pita.

But why do I recall this all?

Maybe the really real question is, Why do I want to know why I recall this in the first place?

Can't I just enjoy this breakfast, all these years later, a breakfast after an overnight flight from Prague where I've spent two weeks teaching at a writer's conference, before me two more weeks of teaching here in Jerusalem, this time teachers of English and literature sponsored by the U.S. State Department?

Can't I just partake of God's bounty here, in His city? Now, as I write this?

The answer: I put my fork to the first cube of that red red watermelon, a deep and memorable red that will last all these years and more for the promise of it, the crisp cold sweet of it about to arrive, and I bite in.

And oh the beauty of that first taste of Israel, the cool of it, the sweetness, the promise fulfilled, and I look up from the plate in this restaurant to the majesty of those walls across the little valley—not much more than a ravine—between us, and the cascade of low white buildings on the forested sides of Mt. Zion, atop it that belltower, that blue round roof.

"Is everything good?" the waiter quietly says, suddenly here beside me. He's still smiling, nods his head, his hands on his hips now, his once-turned cuffs crisp, sharp. "Perhaps more coffee?"

"Everything is great," I say, and glance down at my plate, then back up. "Can I have a cappuccino?"

"Of course," he says, and nods again, reaches to the empty espresso cup and saucer and takes it, nods again.

"Toda," I say, and he says, "Bevakasha," and smiles, heads away.

A tear off the pita next, a drag with it in the hummus and olive oil and pine nuts and that green spice, all of it creamy, and savory, and chewy, and beautiful, the earth and all its bounty here at once, and already the waiter is back, sets the cappuccino down, the foam in a leaf pattern.

"Toda," I say yet again, and now the truth of how little of the language I have is fully revealed, me just a dumb automaton. But the waiter still smiles, says, "Bevakasha," and nods, starts to turn.

So to cover my dullness, to make it seem maybe I might be a little more engaging—actually, maybe a little smarter than I really am—I say, "So bevakasha means please and you're welcome both?"

He turns back to me, gives a small shrug. "Ken," he says, still as quiet as ever. Then he puts a hand to the chair across from me, the other hand on his hip, crosses one foot over the other, the toe of his shoe to the ground, like a farmer leaning on a rake to take a break.

He's going to stay for a moment or so, but I don't mind. There is no one else here. It is early morning in Jerusalem. Here on my plate is the bounty of this place, and I make my confession.

"This is my first time here," I say. "In Israel. And I've already used up all the words I know," and I give a small laugh.

He shrugs, that hand at his hip out now, palm up. He dips his head one way and the other. "You are doing good," he says, still in that near-whisper, still with that space between each word: You. Are. Doing. Good. He puts the hand back to his hip, dips his head again, and says, "You can use other words." He pauses, shrugs. "In Arabic, shukran mean thank you. You are welcome, afwan." He shrugs again. "Is different way to say." He smiles.

I smile, nod.

Something has happened here. Something good. But it will take a while before I can see what it is.

Maybe not until now, writing this down, at the beginning of this book about food and place and people, and being a human, and wondering why I remember this all.

I know something more now, sitting at my table with this cappuccino, this plate of watermelon and eggs and pita and hummus. Something that has made this new world in which I have arrived even larger but, strangely, even smaller with the dimbulb recognition there are two languages here.

Za'atar is the name of the green spice with sesame seeds sprinkled across the hummus, I will one day find out. It's the lingering taste I taste here in the midst of learning these new words; it's what has given the creamy hummus its earthy sense, the forest I can taste just above its lemon hint. It is the *here* of here I can still taste.

I lift up the cappuccino, hold it in a kind of toast to its arrival. "Shukran," I say.

"Afwan," he nods, and makes yet again the sweeping gesture with his arm to the table, and the food before me, and then he is gone.

I take a sip: warm, bitter, soft.

Here are the walls of Jerusalem. Here is Mt. Zion. Here are new words.

I take another tear of the pita, another dab at the hummus. I take another taste of here.

Shmuel, Mishkenot, the Judean Hills

OF COURSE THERE IS more to arriving in Israel that first morning of the breakfast buffet and the view out to old walls. The all of that arrival remains swathed in a kind of mystery, a kind of magic that resides in me still.

Maybe it was the lack of sleep. Or the unfolding foreignness of everything, or the way the sun broke against the Judean hills that early morning.

But I won't forget it. Because I was going up to Jerusalem.

The overnight flight from Prague meant showing up at the airport at 10:00 p.m. I'd spent the day wrapping up the workshop I'd been leading, a graduate creative writing class offered through Western Michigan University. There'd been the workshops nearly every day the last two weeks, readings most every night, lectures by local writers and professors, faculty meetings, one-on-one meetings with each student in my class, meetings and meetings. All that.

Work. But, yes, work in Prague, in the old town—Staré Město—with its broad and cobblestoned town square ringed by elegantly pastel buildings shoulder to shoulder, flat-fronted and tall, like soldiers lined up for inspection. Cafes everywhere, their outdoor tables beneath awnings advertising Pilsner Urquell and Segafredo, and there was the astronomical clock where hundreds of tourists—me included—knotted up to watch the ancient carved-wood apostles march out on the hour.

But even though I'd spent the last two weeks in Prague with all its utterly European charms, I was still tired. I showed up at the airport intending to sleep as much of the nearly four-hour flight as I could, maybe even catch a snooze while waiting at the gate.

That did not happen. I sat at the gate, my green Jansport backpack and old leather briefcase in hand, got on board, took my seat, and stayed awake.

Because I was going to Israel—to Israel! How could I have even thought I might sleep? So I sat there, and watched the night out my window.

Until finally a thin line of deep deep orange appeared on the horizon, above it magenta feeding off into a kind of gray into blue and a darker blue. The pilot announced, first in Czech, then in English, our initial descent, and the plane made that smallest of small moves down, our approach begun.

Next came the general hubbub of an airplane once that descent starts: the cabin lights shuddered on, overhead bins clicked open, slammed shut. Flight attendants passed out customs entry forms, and a murmur replaced the quiet I hadn't known was there while the cabin had been dark, and I'd watched the sky go from black to this thought of a sunrise.

It was only 4:00 in the morning.

The fact I was even headed to Israel started back in 1981, when I went off to UMass Amherst for grad school, and there, in class one night, met a guy named Michael Richards.

The rest is history. Michael went off to join the State Department, while I went off to teach remedial English at Ohio State University, and to try and become a writer. We stayed in touch now and again over the years—he was living around the world while I moved on to teach in Charleston, South Carolina, where Melanie and I grew our family—until one day in 2003 I got an invitation to come to Israel, be a part of a program through the American Cultural Center that taught high school teachers from around the country how to teach American literature, maybe even a little creative writing too.

It wouldn't be until 2005 that I could make it, 2004 taken up with our moving to Baton Rouge after eighteen years at the College of Charleston. I'd been offered the job of editor and director of *The Southern Review*, the storied literary journal founded by Robert Penn Warren and Cleanth Brooks at LSU, and so any idea of taking time away that year was gone. The next year, the gigs in Prague and Israel butted up nicely with each other to make one solid month of teaching, and Melanie would meet me at the end of it all so that we might spend our own time exploring the country.

By this time, though, Michael had already been reassigned. He was in South Korea now, and we wouldn't see each other for eight more years. But it would be in Israel.

Then here came this predawn summer morning, and a horizon.

My passport and entry form in hand, I filed off the plane with everyone else, and we walked, and walked, down glass corridor after glass corridor after glass corridor. Like every airport, the halls were lined with advertise-ments: stylized black and white cows against a blue sky dotted with cartoon clouds, young people smiling with telephones to their ears, a man with his hands up in surprise at a list of symbols beside him.

Even in Prague, with its signage and street names and menus in Czech, I could feel as though I might come close to understanding what I read, no matter if I were correct or not. That letter there was an A, whether in English or Czech. That one was an R, that one an E. I could guess the sound of each cluster of words, pronounce it in my head, recognize it as a word.

But here on all these signs were only rows of what looked like lines and dashes, broken Cs and snubbed off Ns and squeezed Ws, but not even that. Just lines, all jammed into rows, like too many people in a queue pushed into small groups too close together.

I'd arrived in Israel, my first impression that of being at a loss to un-derstand anything. Perhaps that cow was about a dairy product, and I could maybe guess the two kids on phones was about, well, phones. Maybe. But the guy surprised at the words beside him? No clue.

Still we walked, until at some point the corridor circled one story above a food court and fountain, and as we passed we all looked through the glass at the coffee concessions down there, and the restaurants and candy kiosks and boutiques, all of them closed for how early we were.

Then the glass corridors ended, and suddenly we were in a giant hall, thirty feet wide and perhaps a hundred yards long, the ceiling fifty feet above us. The marble floor was angled down, the hall a long ramp from the second floor to the first, the left wall glass from floor to ceiling. Deep brown hills lay in shadow far away out there, above them the sky grown pink and gray.

At the foot of the ramp loomed a wall of limestone up to that high ceiling, hung upon it three framed mosaics, huge and ancient, edges and corners missing. Two square ones on the right, one atop the other, the one on the left long and narrow, all in geometric patterns, with rows of birds inside diamonds on one, a woman holding what looked like a shawl before her on another, the long one a series of circles top to bottom, inside each one a different animal, birds and oxen and horses. All of it in tiny pieces of white and red and green and black, archaeological gems displayed upon the wall like an offering from the country for your simply having entered it.

A giant space. A humbling space. A beautiful and moving space.

Below the wall, at the bottom of the ramp, stood a bank of dark glass doors, above it a lighted sign in Hebrew and English: Passenger Control. We all walked down the ramp, that wall and its mosaics growing closer and more impressive and humbling with each step until, only a few yards before the doors, I looked down to see a man standing to the far left, just before the door in.

He was facing us all, and wore a light blue short-sleeved dress shirt tucked neatly into black pants. He was heavy, balding with thick black eyebrows, and had a lanyard around his neck, a photo ID of some sort hanging from it.

The only person down there, we passengers this school of fish swimming downstream toward him.

He waved at me.

Now he was nodding, took a step toward me, and I slowed, because it seemed I was supposed to know him. I'd been told someone would meet me, but we weren't even to Passport Control, or Customs, or even out in whatever space was beyond it all, where, I'd supposed, a man in a black suit would be holding a small sign with the word LOTT printed on it.

"Mr. Bret?" he said.

I stopped, finally. "Yes?" I said, my own question.

"I am Shmuel," he said, "your driver. I will take you to—" and out came a couple words too fast and too strange for me to understand, his accent heavy, his voice a kind of raspy rusted metal. "Miss Jackie meeting you later today," he said. "I take your backpack?"

"I'm okay," I said, and shrugged it a little higher over my shoulder, nodded. Jackie: Cultural Program Specialist at the American Center. The round-the-clock director of the whole program. We'd be meeting later today, once I'd gotten to the hotel and slept for a few hours.

"Give to me your passport," Shmuel said, and held out a hand. "Entry form too," he said and, dutifully, I handed both to him, and glanced down at that photo ID on his lanyard.

Yes, at least according to the ID, he was with the American Consulate, the State Department seal there with his picture, his name.

Still, for a long fleeting moment, I wondered if this is how it happens, how somebody suddenly disappears in a foreign country.

He was already turned, headed off to the left and the farthest open door. I followed him inside to a booth with a uniformed man inside, glass protecting him from us. I looked over my shoulder to my right, saw all the others headed away to a bank of other glass booths, more men in uniform. Shmuel said something, and I looked back, saw he was speaking to the agent in the booth. He set my passport and form on the counter, passed them through the little opening in the glass. He and the guard both looked at me, said nothing, faces blank, and I gave a smile, nodded, like my manners might solve a problem.

The border agent, still with his eyes on me, said something back to Shmuel, then looked down at my passport, the form, my passport again. He stamped a piece of paper, slipped it into the passport, and handed both the form and passport back. He spoke to Shmuel again, his eyes on me now, then looked at Shmuel, nodded, and Shmuel was off again, past the booth.

"Thank you!" I called out to the agent, perhaps because I wanted him to see in me no threat. Or maybe because I wanted him to see me and remember that nice American guy just before he disappeared.

Next we were at yet another row of agents inside booths, and again Shmuel led us to the farthest one to the left, all the action still off to the right, where rows of arriving passengers were lined up, and for the first moment I let in a sense that, maybe, this was pretty cool, this quick-walk through all the passport stuff. Having a driver. And Shmuel. What a name. Samuel. Shmuel.

This was cool.

The same procedure again, words passed between this next agent and Shmuel, all eyes on me, a stamp, then off through another hallway until we were at baggage claim with its shiny rows of oblong carousels.

We were the first ones there.

Shmuel hustled off to the left yet again, no words from him at all, and we stopped at the end of a carousel, right where the ramp would deposit the bags. He already knew which carousel would be mine.

Yes. Very cool.

I tried small talk on him, and he gave quick smiles, nods, a word or two, and I realized it was still only 5:00 in the morning here, this man pulled out of bed by the job of picking me up.

He lived in Jerusalem. He'd worked as a driver for the American Center for years. It was okay that he had to get up so early. "For me, no problem," he said, and shrugged, gave yet another quick smile.

And as if he had some strange authority over all things—he'd gotten to stand out in the hall with its mosaics and wait for me, had gotten through two sets of agents while all the other passengers piled up into their lines—my black rolling duffel slipped off the ramp and onto the carousel, the first piece of luggage to land in Israel.

I reached for it, but Shmuel took it before I could even touch it, popped out the handle, and we headed past the customs agents at the far end of the complex. Shmuel nodded to them—this guy was a regular regular here, I realized, a kind of celebrity for how many people he seemed to know—and I hurried to stay up with him, opaque white automatic exit doors opening for him. We were the first people out.

Here was yet another massive room, even more glass and more light: the reception hall. We walked across open space, a half-circle maybe a hundred feet across bordered by a low glass wall to separate friends and family and black-suited drivers holding surnames written on paper for the arriving friends and family and those needing a driver.

But mine was already with me. Mine was an inside man, a super-driver. The driver to know.

He was walking even faster now, me trying to stay up with him. A scattering of people stood along the glass wall, some holding balloons, some with flowers, some with arms crossed. Hasidic men in fedoras and bowlers and tendril sidecurls, their wives in drab dresses and herding children; young people in T-shirts and sunglasses and jeans tight as pantyhose, scarves round their necks, messenger bags strapped across chests; people in plaid shirts and khakis.

They all watched us, the first two out of customs, and I couldn't help but feel the self-conscious burn, we two not who anyone here expected. Maybe this was why Shmuel walked so fast: to get through all the scrutiny offered by everyone we'd encountered thus far. But I brushed that off, because I knew Shmuel was just doing his job very early one morning.

We made it through the gantlet, and once we were beyond them all and almost to the glass doorway out, Shmuel pulled off to the left yet one more time, then stopped and turned to me.

"You need money?" he said, more a statement than a question, and nodded to his left, and I looked, saw a row of ATMs.

He was good.

The air outside was warm already, a little humid. This was July, and this was the coast, the Mediterranean only a few miles east. Of course the car, black, shiny, new, was parked only a few feet down the sidewalk out front of the airport, Shmuel with the trunk open and loading in the duffel before I could even offer to do it myself, though there would have been no doing it myself. This was Shmuel.

I sat in the back as directed, and we left, the exit from the airport a wide sweeping curve away toward what looked like a freeway up ahead. Out my window I could see in the morning twilight manicured rows of orange trees, dark and waxy green. Out Shmuel's window lay a vast parking area, beyond it all and still far away the Judean hills.

What else could I do but marvel at even the most mundane of things as we drove? Here were oranges out my window, but they were oranges in Israel; here was a freeway we entered, but a freeway in Israel, traffic light and fast, but fast light traffic in Israel.

The all of it looked, I thought as I took it all in, and though it felt a bit like sin to think so because this was Israel, a lot like southern California. Like Orange County, where I'd grown up, with its dusty brown hills over there, and with these orange trees, and with this freeway and the speed of the cars. A lot like Orange County. But I didn't let myself think this much longer, only pushed it down and behind me, because those hills way over there weren't the Santa Ana Mountains out past Irvine. This was Israel, and these were the Judean hills.

We drove, Shmuel faster than most everyone else, passing car after car after car, and in the early morning gray I could see the hills growing closer to my left, the land widening out to my right, fields now, the flat plain leading away to the sea. And in the distance out there, to the right and miles away like some giant mechanical ghost in the haze of the early morning air, stood what looked like an electrical plant.

Lights, towers, an angular structure settled miles away there on the horizon to the west, where the sky above it was darker. A power plant. Just like the one at the end of Newland Avenue where it hit Pacific Coast Highway in Huntington Beach, the giant green Edison plant with its smokestacks sitting right there on PCH. A mile and a half from our house up at Adams and Newland. Just like it.

I graduated from Edison High School, home of the Chargers. A school named after a power plant.

This place looked just like home.

I leaned forward in my seat, said to Shmuel, because it struck me as somehow strange to see a power plant in the Holy Land, and maybe because I just wanted him to think I wasn't a silent passenger, someone too important to speak to him, "Is that a power plant over there? Way off over there."

"Yes," he said. "Is in Ashdod." He gave a quick shrug. "Near Ashdod."

And then, suddenly, the power plant became an exotic element on the landscape. Yes, it was still a power plant like the one on PCH across the street from the beach, where after school we'd drive down and park and body surf in the afternoon, or just lay out and relax.

But *this* power plant was in Ashdod. The city where the Philistines brought the captured Ark of the Covenant and set it up in Dagon's temple, and where the next morning Dagon's priests found his statue fallen over in front of the ark, and where, after they set him back up, the next morning they found the statue tipped over again, but this time with its hands and head broken off.

Then came the tumors, and Ashdod's packing off the ark for the next Philistine town to deal with.

That Ashdod.

I leaned closer to the window, the kid in me and the writer too who loved the Old Testament stories for their action, their mystery, their terror and redemption fired up now. Ashdod. Right over there.

Only a power plant that looked like the one my high school was named after.

But the kid in me still leaned close to the window, looking.

A few minutes later the freeway curled off to the left, away from the plains and toward a valley, on either side of the road up there hillsides like those beside the freeway up into the San Gabriel Mountains above San Bernardino: rocky, dark green scrub, dry. And then, just before the road turned fully into the valley, came a cluster of green trees, and out my window stood a two-story stone house, square, with a small Moorish window in the wall facing us. It looked old, abandoned, with those trees beside it, green weeds up against it.

The first old building I'd seen thus far, the first sign of antiquity, the first possible sighting of maybe a place from Bible days.

Then it was gone, just like that, and I said to Shmuel, "What was that? That old building?"

His eyes on the road, he said something fast, a couple words too quick to decipher, then, "Is old caravan stop. Means 'Gate of the Valley.'" He paused, looked in his side view, gassed it and passed another car. The hillsides beside us were closer in now, still in morning twilight. "This is old road to Jerusalem."

A caravan stop. The Gate of the Valley. The old road to Jerusalem.

I saw camels, a star in the sky to the east, gifts of the Magi. I saw a woman on a donkey being led by a man with a walking stick, all of it in shadow against a night sky, maybe on that ridge up there out my window. I saw David looking down on Goliath in a valley that couldn't be far from here, and asking why no one was down there taking on this braggart, this blowhard. No matter he was a giant. I saw Daniel in the lion's den—but wait, that was in Babylon, a long way away.

Shmuel passed another car, and another.

The sky was growing lighter now, the hillsides beside us given more detail, though still they looked like the hillsides on I-15 headed for the Cajon Pass in the San Gabriel Mountains. There were trees down here at the bottom of the valley, pine and cypress, it looked like, maybe some oak too. Bushes up the hillsides beside us, a few trees too.

Very much like California.

But then I saw out my window an old abandoned truck, an *ancient* abandoned truck, rusted red completely, no tires, no glass, no nothing. Just the empty shell of an abandoned truck. A very very old abandoned truck.

Huh. Couldn't the country see its way to towing off junk like this? A truck that had to have been there for decades, judging by the rust. Something you'd find under a tarp, long forgotten in the back of a barn.

But here was another one, and now I noticed the body of it, up at the cab at least, looked more like metal plates for doors and the roof than any old jalopy of a truck I'd seen before. Then came another just like it, right here out my window for all the world to see, and I leaned forward in my seat, asked Shmuel—Shmuel! What a great name!—"Why are these old trucks out here?"

He leaned his head a little one way, then the other, and I couldn't get a read on whether he were tired of me and my idiot questions, or if maybe he had to think about this one for a second.

"Is transport trucks. Military," he finally said. "Memorial. These trucks destroyed in convoy to Jerusalem in war. Nineteen and forty-eight." He paused. "Is here to remember."

Oh.

I eased back in my seat, and took that in. Just as here came another one, rusted red, stripped bare, just out there, trees behind it, but easy to see from here on the road. Meant to be seen from here on the road.

Meant to be a reminder, no matter how many times you drove this road. Meant to inform, too, no matter how naïve you were. Like me.

Left there to make you ask questions if you didn't know, and remember if you did.

So what did I know about Israel before coming here?

War, mostly. Beyond the Bible, I only knew what I'd seen on the news since I was a kid. I knew the Six Day War only as a vague memory. I was only nine in 1967, and more worried about my paper route than the headlines of the papers I was throwing from the canvas bag on my handlebars. But my mom subscribed to *Life*, and I remember seeing a cover with an Israeli soldier in water—the Suez Canal, the cover read—smiling in the bright sun and with a beat-up rifle in his hand, inside the issue all kinds of pictures of the war, and how much a miracle it was the Israelis had won. There was what happened at the Munich Olympics too, after the glory of Mark Spitz and his seven gold medals, and Olga Korbut and her three: the terrorists breaking into the athletes' village. I remember watching it all on television, and me being old enough to be astonished that this was going on, that terrorists had taken athletes. I remember watching that one man in the gray ski mask coming out onto the balcony and looking back and forth, and the commentators all totally confused about how this could be happening. And then all the athletes killed, and the even greater astonishment that the Olympics just went right on.

I'd seen pictures of the war in October 1973, too, another short one but with lots of photos in *Life* again. I'd watched the bombings through the years after that, the buses in flames, the homes bulldozed. I'd heard of peace and peace again, seen Jimmy Carter and Anwar Sadat and Menachem Begin all shaking hands at Camp David, then Bill Clinton and Yasser Arafat and Ehud Barak at Camp David. I'd seen Sadat shot by his own troops during that parade, Itzhak Rabin assassinated by one of his own countrymen, and Yasser Arafat always lying low but riding high, outlasting them all.

And not long after Michael Richards had contacted me in 2003, asked me to come to Israel and teach, give some readings, meet people, I'd watched the news about those three Israeli soldiers abducted by Hezbollah up on the Lebanon border while UN peacekeepers watched, and then seen the news about their dead bodies being returned in exchange for a few hundred Palestinian and Lebanese prisoners and the bodies of their comrades.

So I knew a few things.

And somewhere along the line when I was a kid I'd watched a pretty bad movie that starred Kirk Douglas as an American officer who decides to join in with the Israeli army in 1948. John Wayne was in it, a general who was Kirk Douglas's commanding officer and didn't want to let him go to Israel to fight but who, well, looks the other way. Yul Brenner was in it too, as this slightly sinister Israeli who might not trust Kirk, at least at first.

And then Kirk—the general running this ragtag bunch of excited but inexperienced soldiers—gets killed. By friendly fire.

They were building a road, I remembered. One to get around the road through a valley up to Jerusalem. Where convoys kept getting hammered from the hillsides by Arab troops.

This road. The road where the Israeli fighters were getting killed, trying to save Jerusalem and the people in it.

These rusted out trucks, these here, were the vehicles destroyed trying to get there, through this valley. Before they finished that road around it all to outflank the Arab soldiers firing down on these doomed trucks, and those inside them.

I stayed quiet for a while then, just looked out my window watching for the chance to see any more of those trucks, those memorials.

The hillsides loomed higher beside us, and as we drove I could see that the hills began to be terraced, shelf after shelf up the sides, and I could make out too that there were olive trees growing on those terraces. The road twisted and kept going up, then came to a kind of crest, and I could see buildings off to the left, a town of some sort over there, the sun very nearly up now, but all still in shadow, and then the road went down into another valley. Traffic began to pick up a bit, and at times the terraces disappeared and gave way to what seemed like striations on the hillsides, thin rock layers of a sort, lining the hills by the dozens, the hundreds. Little strips of rock the length of a hillside, each of which looked no more than an inch or two thick and maybe a foot or two apart from each other, all up the sides. Between each rock line lay the earth, brown, and scrub brush, maybe the thought of grass, though this was July.

I broke my self-imposed silence then, and leaned forward again, asked, "What are those lines on the hillsides?"

"What?" he said, and though his eyes were on the road—we were passing yet another car—I could see a small wince of puzzlement: What is this guy talking about? Why is he asking so many questions?

"On the hillside," I said. "There's little lines. Little rock layers back and forth."

He glanced away from the road, ducked a little to see out the windshield to his right and the hillside. He sat back, eyes forward again. "Is sheep lines. Sheep trails." He paused, smiled at the thought, I knew even as he gave it, that this American would be intrigued even by sheep trails.

But sheep trails. In Israel, on the road to Jerusalem. Hundreds of them, worn in over thousands of years.

Here was David again, the boy out tending the herd because his dad, Jesse, didn't think the prophet Samuel—Shmuel?—would miss his youngest when he came looking to anoint God's replacement for Saul.

I was a kid looking out a car window at hills striated with trails, and happy with that.

This was when, up at the top, along the ridge up there, dawn finally broke onto the hilltops, the rocks up there a sudden sharp gold, the scrub bushes up there suddenly articulate in their light and shadow, green and brown and gray. Then came an olive tree into the light, and another, all of them impossibly olive-green green.

The sky above it a blue past words.

A few minutes later we were at the outer edges of Jerusalem. Buildings started sprouting, long low ones and taller ones, too, all square with flat roofs and tiered streets where homes perched on the valley walls. The freeway rose up the hillside to the right, hugged it, curved to the right and right, and suddenly here were vast stone bulkheads tiered up the hill, encasing it in stone walls twenty and thirty feet high all the way to the top, and what other recourse did I have, this rube of all rubes, this American pest in the back seat, than to lean forward and ask Shmuel, "What is that? Those walls?"

"Is cemetery. Jewish cemetery." He drove on.

Oh.

Buildings started becoming high-rises, the freeway still slung along the hillside, traffic heavier, the valley to the left giving way to rolling hills carpeted with low-lying buildings—homes?—until the freeway held right through one more curve, and there stood the city on a hill.

Apartment buildings, mainly, and other buildings too, what seemed offices, spired at the top of the hill. Shmuel finally left the freeway, and we snaked our way through hushed streets packed with homes and parks, high-rise condos and townhouses. The road led up and up, on the streets here and there people dressed the same as those at the airport, Hasidim and tourists and the terminally hip alike, but not many, and most walking with heads down, quick on their way somewhere else.

This was a city, waking up at dawn on a July morning.

We crested the hill. The streets had sidewalks, most of the homes with limestone walls waist high and a foot thick out front. Trees shrouded much of what I could see of their yards, and sometimes atop the limestone walls were wrought iron fences. The yards were small, blocky, everything in squares, like adobes but of limestone, the trees and growth shrouding doorways and windows.

Shmuel gunned it down the hill, swung the car through a traffic circle, those homes giving way to hotels and offices, all limestone, all white, and then we were at a large intersection, a hotel to the right, a park across the street on the downhill side and facing east into that sun still low in the sky. We waited, and then the red light turned a blinking yellow—what was that about?—then a moment later green, and in the instant between that yellow to green, a horn honked behind us, and another.

But it didn't matter. Shmuel was already on the move.

We pulled through the intersection and into the park. Shmuel finally slowed down, the narrow street lined with olive trees and rosemary bushes, cypress trees too, and there, straight ahead and as out of place as a huge Dutch windmill in Jerusalem, stood a huge Dutch windmill.

All limestone, full-sized—it had to be fifty feet tall—with four blades, no sails on any of them but only the metal frames, the cap dark bronze, it looked like, or maybe copper.

A windmill.

Before I could even lean forward to ask, Shmuel said, "Montefiore Windmill. Eighteen and fifty seven." He glanced at me in the rear-view mirror. "This is Yemen Moshe. We are almost there."

"Wow" was all I said, and sat back.

The street ended at the base of the windmill—a windmill—turned right, and Shmuel eased down the hill, then left onto a small curl of a street, to my left a limestone wall, to the right out my window the hillside falling into another valley. From here I could see far away, to the east. There were hills lower than this over there, and beyond them in the distance more mountains. Very far away.

Now here was an iron gate before us, and Shmuel stopped the car.

"We are here," he said and paused, then spoke two words. It took me a moment, but I realized they were the same ones he'd said when I'd first met him at the bottom of that ramp beneath the mosaics: *I am Shmuel, your driver. I will take you to—*

This was it. Mishkenot Sha'ananim. The guest house where I'd be staying. Those were the words he'd spoken, come to me as they should be pronounced, and not the dull second-grade sounding out in my head I'd used whenever I read the words in correspondences from Jackie: *Mish-key-not Shah-ah-nah-nim.*

Of course those were the words he'd said back at the airport. Where else would he have been taking me?

"Great," I said, and now something was coming to me, some kind of kindling fear for the fact Shmuel would be leaving me here soon. My superdriver. My guide. The man whose mere presence expedited luggage so that mine was the first bag off. The one who'd given me, this kid at a car window and in so very few words, my introduction to this extraordinary place.

I looked at him in the rear-view. "Thanks for putting up with me," I said. "All my questions."

"It is okay," he said, and smiled, the edge now of that rusted metal voice somehow a little sanded down.

The iron gate opened then, and he pulled through, the street still curving down to the left, the valley to the right filled with this early morning light.

But for a moment I thought I caught to the left a glimpse of a hill closer in than I'd seen from where we'd sat waiting for the gates to open. A promontory, maybe.

And a white belltower on it, white buildings in a kind of cascade down the forested hillside over there.

Just ahead stood the guest house, low and flat and limestone, the street now become a cul-de-sac, the glass doors into Mishkenot Sha'ananim at its end. In a few minutes I'd be in my room, where double doors let out onto a covered porch, and a view. A little while later, I'd be in the restaurant and marveling at a breakfast buffet, and meet a waiter who would teach me new ways to say thank you.

But for now Shmuel only pulled the car to a stop at the end of the cul-de-sac, popped open his door and had my black duffel out all before I could close my own door. I pulled my backpack onto one shoulder, my briefcase in hand, and followed him in.

It was in this way I'd gone up to Jerusalem.

On *Za'atar*

ONE DAY NOT LONG after we'd moved to Jerusalem, Melanie and I were just inside Jaffa Gate, the arched limestone entrance into the western side of the Old City. We'd spent the afternoon walking the quarters in some sort of preamble to our later solo travel into wider and wider circles out from this center. The summer before, during our first visit, we'd had a guide, a voluble and goofy and incredibly intelligent young Russian named Mickey, who'd shown us all over the city and out as far as Qumran and the Dead Sea. But now we were on our own.

Melanie was taking photos of the gate, and the Tower of David near it, the limestone tower all the world like a medieval castle you'd see in an Errol Flynn movie. Something David himself never laid eyes on, the walls and tower built by the Mamluk sultan al-Nasir Muhammad only after the crusaders had been cleared out.

So I was standing, watching, and saw there, just inside the gate, a kid beside a cart, a beat-up square green thing with bicycle tires for wheels.

But what lay atop it was what got me: a couple rows of big elongated bread rings, foot-long crosses between bagels and soft pretzels, sesame seeds baked into the tops. They looked sort of exotic, and maybe tasty, and pretty easy to tote. And I was hungry.

So I took a step toward the cart.

Before I could say a word, me still four or five paces from contact, the kid—he couldn't have been more than ten, his hair buzzcut, shirt too big—zeroed in on me, said, "Five shekels," and held up his hand, all five fingers extended in case I needed a visual aid.

"I'd like two, bevakasha," I said, and he gave a smile, nodded hard. He picked out two, with the other hand reached somewhere inside the cart and brought out a small black plastic grocery sack, loaded them in.

"Toda," I said, and handed him a ten-shekel bill. He gave me the bag, nodded again, smiling, and started to stuff the bill in his pocket.

But then he stopped, quick-turned to look behind him, and I realized someone was talking to him.

There on the stoop of the building behind him—a shop of some sort—sat a man in jeans and a striped polo who looked just like the kid. He was leaned back on his elbows on the steps, feet crossed in front of him, taking it easy. A dad, his son working the cart for a while.

He said something to the kid again, who shrugged, then looked into where he'd pulled that bag out, retrieved something else, and held out his hand to me.

Two small triangle-shaped parcels, the same size as the paper footballs we made in seventh grade and flicked back and forth between us during study period. Made of what looked like newsprint, off-white, compact, and I slowly put out my free hand to take whatever they were.

"He forget give you," the man said from the stoop, and I looked at him. He was smiling, and nodded. "My boy new on this job."

I laughed then, nodded, and the kid dropped the two triangles in my hand. I nodded at the kid, the man. "He's doing a great job!" I said to him.

I dropped the triangles into the bag with the bread, turned to look for Melanie somewhere around here, in me no clue what these little packets held.

The bread rings were called Jerusalem bagels, I found out not long after from one of my grad students, though—as ever—there were plenty enough names to go around: Israeli bread, Palestinian bread, *Ka'ak*. And that same grad student would tell me never to pay more than three shekels for one, five for two.

But once Melanie and I made the twenty-minute walk that afternoon from the Old City back to our apartment in German Colony, and I took a bite of that bread ring—chewy, but baked, not boiled like a bagel, a little nutty for the sesame seeds, maybe even just a whisper of sweet in there too—I wouldn't care what it was called or if I'd overpaid a little. I loved it.

Then I fished one of the packets from the bottom of the bag, carefully unfolded it on the kitchen table as though it were some sort of secret message found at a dead drop.

And there it was, a good solid tablespoon of dark green herbs and spices and sesame seeds.

Za'atar.

This was supposed to go with the ring. So important an element of Jerusalem bagels a father had to watch over his son to make sure he passed it along.

I tore off another piece, pushed it into the spice, and took a bite. Even better.

Later still, I'd figure out to dip the bread first in olive oil, then in *za'atar*, and that combo became solid gold.

It's all about the *za'atar*.

There's an etymological descriptor for the kind of word *za'atar* is: a loan-word. Which means exactly what you think, a word loaned out from elsewhere and grown into another language. And though you don't hear the word *za'atar* bandied about in American kitchens like you do mustard (French, an easy one) or ketchup (Chinese) or even coleslaw (Dutch), it's a pretty common—very common—loanword in the middle east. Because it's everywhere.

It's an Arabic word, loaned out to Hebrew, and the spice mixture is used on pretty much anything. But it's also a valued element of a dish, not a throwaway spice sprinkled over something for the sake of tradition. I've put it on chicken and steak and every roasted vegetable you can think of, on scrambled, fried and hard-boiled eggs, on pizza and salad and sometimes in the morning simply on a piece of toast with olive oil. And every time it tastes like *za'atar*, and everything tastes *more* for it. Whereas when you put salt in a dish that needs more salt, and you taste it—and provided you've added the right amount of salt—you'll say, Better.

But when you add *za'atar*, you'll say, There.

The taste: dark, green, a little bitter. A forest, lemon. An old taste, as in a taste past time, a hearkening back to some other place.

The earth.

There's also a murkiness in its meaning and its common usage in that *za'atar* is both an herb *and* the spice mixture. The herb itself—*origanum syriacum*—lives throughout the middle east, and looks something a little like lavender in that it grows on stalks with leaves that same pale gray-green, though they are broader, bigger, more like stubby sage than anything else. But *za'atar* the spice mixture doesn't always contain *za'atar* the herb. Sort of like how a Kleenex is always a tissue, but a tissue isn't always a Kleenex. Yeah, like that.

I think.

Or how about this: Oftentimes you'll find in *za'atar the spice mixture* dried marjoram and/or oregano and/or thyme, but no *za'atar the herb.* Sometimes there'll be dried lemon or orange zest in there too, and dill now and again, even caraway seeds and cumin. But the real thing is made simply of *za'atar* the herb, those toasted sesame seeds, ground sumac (with its gloriously rich burgundy hue), a little bit of sea salt, and a dash of olive oil.

Things get even more involved the deeper you dig into that etymology. The Classical Hebrew word for *za'atar* in the Bible is *ezov,* which, when it was translated into the Greek, became the word ὕσσωπος: hyssop. And now, in this moment of words on a page, *za'atar's* surprise in my triangular newsprint football dropped into my hands by a boy selling bread suddenly multiplies in manifold and mysterious ways, its primary ingredient and namesake in the herb mixture the tool for painting lamb's blood on doorframes the first Passover; it becomes the means by which one is cleansed, whether from leprosy in Leviticus or the deepest reaches of sin ("Cleanse me with hyssop, and I will be clean; wash me, and I will be whiter than snow," David cries out in Psalm 51); in 1 Kings it becomes an element of the wisdom of Solomon. ("He spoke three thousand proverbs and his songs numbered a thousand and five. He spoke about plant life, from the cedar of Lebanon to the hyssop that grows out of walls.")

And the Gospel of John tells us of its role in quenching Christ's thirst as He hung there on the cross, the sour wine one last moment of earthly relief before His work here is complete:

> After this, Jesus, knowing that all was now finished, said (to fulfill the Scripture), "I thirst." A jar full of sour wine stood there, so they put a sponge full of the sour wine on a hyssop branch and held it to his mouth. When Jesus had received the sour wine, he said, "It is finished," and he bowed his head and gave up his spirit.

Somehow, in this tablespoonful of green and bitter herbs mixed with other spices and seeds, I am partaking of the history of my faith, tasting time and place and salvation.

It is a marvelous flavor.

Eleven years later, after living here and all our stays thereafter, Melanie and I are on our first bus tour of Israel, riding in one of those giant rectangular ships that swarm the country, no matter where you are.

But this is not your typical land cruise. This one's been dubbed by we participants the Magical Mystery Tour. A cliché, sure, but we're all okay with that.

We're a gathering of artists, writers, musicians and most all our spouses. Sixteen of us, including Or, our gangly, shaved-headed, six-foot-four guide who, in his long-sleeve plaid shirts and ubiquitous backpack, forever on his head a gray thin-brimmed sun hat, is hipster hip. But he wears it like the sabra he is, the Israeli-born among the citizenry, known for their calm and sharp-eyed sense of humor.

And there's the one who brought us all here, Luke Moon, a Seattleite in his forties, with his curly salt and pepper hair and matching beard, an easy smile and kind eyes. He's the deputy director of a group called The Philos Project, the New York-based organization that's sponsored this whole thing. The Philos Project is, to quote its mission statement, "a dynamic leadership community dedicated to promoting positive Christian engagement in the Near East," and seeks to share its vision of recognizing the many ethnic, racial, religious, and social groups found here while promoting the common civilization they all share. The project offers its own bespoke educational resources and other opportunities to help leaders in the Christian community simply understand the region in ways they might not otherwise have found. Their final goal is, "A pluralistic Near East based on freedom and the rule of law where nations, tribes, and religious communities can live beside each other as neighbors."

A worthy mission, certainly.

A primary element of the project is to bring groups here for "immersive travel programs" (also in the mission statement) for boots-on-the ground explorations of these issues with people here who live inside them. Luke's told us of bringing American gangs of business leaders, politicians, even sports figures for these tours.

But, he tells us too, he's never brought a bunch of artists with him. He tells us this because, now and again, we get out of hand.

We laugh. A lot. We sing songs. We tell jokes, recite poetry, and we all tell each other stories from our lives. We're hard to herd through what we see and where we go, all of us engaged with and in everything we take in. We talk, and talk, and we laugh. A lot.

Luke laughs along with us, but it's more a soft chuckle, sometimes accompanied by a slow shake of the head, almost ruefully: Who are these people, and why are they making me laugh? And why can't we get them back on the bus?

But there are many times when we all sit and look pensively out our windows, and try as hard as possible to take in all the disparate and complementary info we're receiving. We visit a hospital in the north that takes in wounded Syrian rebels dropped off by their fellow fighters at the border with Israel because they know the Israelis will care for them; we take a briefing on the Palestinian situation with a lead Israeli negotiator who has told us the only way both sides can hold onto things is by giving them up; and we sit in Midron Yaffo Park with its sloping lawn down to the Mediterranean and listen to a Palestinian woman, her family residents of the old port city of Yaffo—Joppa—Jaffa—for untold generations, tell us of how the towering concrete of Tel Aviv to the north creeps relentlessly into this historic place.

From where we sit listening to her we can see the breakwater for the old port of Yaffo, where Jonah began his escape from God by heading out to sea. From where we sit we can see the white belltower of St. Peter's Church, built on the site, it is believed, where Peter stayed at Simon the tanner's house.

But along with these important and moving moments we also have our fun. We spend a day at a resort on the too-warm Dead Sea where first we bob in the water like corks, then get refreshed with a swim in the cool water of the resort pool. In our hotel in Tel Aviv, the morning cappuccini come with happy slogans cocoa-stenciled in the foam ("It's Your Lucky Day!" with, strangely, a drawing of a game of tic-tac-toe; "Good Morning!" with a baby chick chirping); when we're in Jerusalem at the Mamilla Hotel, the breakfast buffet is five times as long as the one at Mishkenot Sha'ananim. We walk the streets of old Jaffa and gaze up at the apartment building where it is rumored Gal Gadot lives or might have lived or is thinking about living.

There's a lot to put together in this tour.

Right now we're headed toward Nazareth from the north, hills easing up to the left, the land falling away little by little to our right. We've spent the last long while driving through the brown and rolling hills above and to the west of the Sea of Galilee, but now that we've turned off bucolic Highway 77 and toward Nazareth, strip malls start crowding in, their parking lots out front. Then the lots end altogether, the shops moving right up to the edge of the street, cars parked out front with tails hanging out.

We're in Kafar Kanna, also spelled Kufr Kana, and probably another way or two I don't yet know. We know it as Cana, where Jesus turned the water into wine at the wedding feast. But it's all these stores and the growing traffic that has our attention: electronics stores and telephone stores and tire stores (why are there so many tire stores?) all bunched up. The street seems to grow narrower for this bus in the middle of it, all of us looking out our windows at these cars everywhere, people walking out there too, and on bicycles and riding scooters and motorcycles and driving these cars.

And though this is Cana and home to that first miracle, we're not heading to the church that stands on the traditional spot where the wedding feast was held, as any predictable Holy Land tour might very well do. We're headed to an olive oil cooperative, where we'll listen to its story and have a tasting of its products.

This is the Magical Mystery Tour.

Suddenly the bus driver takes a right off the highway, and we roll on down a street away from the main drag, the street narrowing even more until it seems the bus will scrape the bumpers right off the cars along here.

Another turn, another, the stores now industrial buildings, limestone warehouses with big bay doors; there's a truck repair shop out there, and a tractor dealership, an open lot with granite and limestone sheets stacked on their sides, and piles of limestone bricks.

Then the bus stops, out the windows to the right a warehouse, green bay doors closed, a fenced lot out front with metal barrels and carts and industrial-looking Other Stuff, a short set of stairs up its left outside wall. Or stands at the front, turns to us all and says, "Okay. We are here," in the deadpan way he does at every place we go. Then we all rise, file off the bus, and head up those steps.

Inside is a quiet and spacious gift shop. Wooden shelves and cabinets line the walls, filled with bottles of olive oils, baskets, soaps, olive wood utensils, jars of honey, candles, even a small jewelry kiosk of sorts. Old wooden cable spools serve as display tables, on them gift boxes of olive oil to carry away or to ship home. It's a nice space, friendly with all its wood everywhere, and the smell of these soaps.

We've been given information about this place already—it's in the program brochure we were issued on our first day with the tour—but perhaps because I'm a bit tired from this long day, or maybe because I'm always a little wary of being brought to gift shops as part of a tour, I'm almost on autopilot at this stop. We're here for an olive oil tasting, which means, yes, an opportunity to purchase products. Hence a perusal of this nice gift shop.

A few minutes later we're lined up for the tasting, held up at the counter where purchases will be made. We'll have to work in shifts, only five or six of us at a time able to fit in and taste the teaspoonful dripped into each tiny plastic cup by the women working the other side of the counter. The first is one of their single-cultivar pressings, the taste full, green, a little peppery, a little keen on the tongue. Excellent. Then a second oil to taste, the house blend: smooth, a little fruity and maybe a little rounder where it lingers at the sides of the tongue. Excellent too! We'll buy some of both to bring home with us, a decision made just like that.

And then we are hustled—in a subtle but certain way—by Or and a woman who seems to work here into a side room, a square space lined with low cushioned benches corner to corner against three walls. There's also a couple tables—plastic, fold-out—to one side with chairs before them. The fourth wall has a sofa of its own, standing in front of it three people: the woman who's gotten us in here, maybe in her forties with long and curly hair, glasses, jeans, and a white smock; a balding man maybe in his thirties in a gray polo with the collar popped; and a second woman, who wears a traditional black abaya and a purple-and gray-checked hijab fit snugly so that we see her face only from the eyebrows down to her chin. She is perhaps the same age as the other woman—it's hard to tell with the hijab so perfectly framing her face—and she doesn't look happy. Stern is more like it.

On the wall behind them hangs a row of three framed posters. The outside two are large photos of women in hijabs and abayas working together. In one two women settle bottles into boxes, in the other three women sit weaving baskets.

The poster in the middle is light green with the white logo I've been seeing on all the goods here. It's a stylized olive tree, hidden in the leaves on either side of the tree the single-line profiles of two female faces. On the left of the tree is something in Arabic, on the right something in Hebrew, and along the bottom the English translation of both, *Sindyanna of Galilee The Taste of Fair Trade*.

Okay. We are here.

The two women sit on their sofa, and the man—I can't catch his name, his Hebrew accent thick but for the most part understandable—tells us a bit about the products, the olives harvested from old Arab groves that have been revitalized over the last twenty years, and the new fields begun over that time as well, all of it certified organic, all according to international Fair Trade practices—Sindyanna has been a member of the World Fair Trade Organization since 2003. He tells us of how the oil was recently awarded an Extra Gold Medal at an international competition in Italy, and that the enterprise continues to grow beyond what anyone involved would have expected. Their oils are served in fine restaurants throughout Israel now, and sell all over Europe; it's available in select Whole Foods markets in the U.S., and Amazon will soon be selling it too.

Then comes the woman in jeans and the smock. Nadia is her name, her job the chief facilitator and manager of the Sindyanna center, and the *story* story of this place genuinely begins.

She tells us in her accented English that the cooperative began when people with foresight, people with imagination, saw a way to bridge the gap between Arab producers and Israeli consumers—and that it was the women here in Galilee, Arab and Israeli alike, who had finally grown tired of the lack of opportunity for anything beyond their roles as housewives. There were tracts of land with old groves on them, and the men involved didn't want to work them for one reason and another—old reasons, reasons beyond genuine memory—and these women came together to make something happen amongst themselves, banded together these lands and began to work toward making something good that would bring money in to support them, especially the Arab women. Next came soaps, and spices, and traditional baskets, all manner of goods produced, packaged, sold, and shipped under Sindyanna's name by the women who work here. It's a nonprofit, all proceeds fed back into the cooperative and its programs for the Arab women it serves.

And the whole thing works.

Then slowly the stern-seeming woman in the abaya and purple-and-gray hajib stands, Nadia serving as her translator, and she tells in Arabic her own story, haltingly, even though she speaks it in her own language. Because it's a very difficult story, a personal one. A story of particular oppressions, of poverty, of no future to head toward or even imagine, but a story that, through finding employment with Sindyanna, has begun to be lived with some sense of light now, some sense of hope. Some sense of good, and as she relays this all to us, Nadia speaking for her, we can see a smile, however timorous, however glancing, now and again when she speaks of this place, and the people here to help.

We are quiet when she finishes, and a moment later several quiet *Thank yous* are murmured among us for her, and then one or another of us claps for her, and we all join in, clapping for her and for the story of this place, its vision. Its desire to create, through agriculture and industry, commerce and hope, something true and good and beautiful.

Luke, sitting on the cushioned bench to my left, is smiling. He has a hand to his chin, his elbow cupped in the palm of his other hand, legs crossed. He's been here a few times before. He's heard these stories. But still, I can tell, he's moved by this, and, like me, like Melanie, like all the others in our group, our herd of cats, right now, here, we are amazed at the notion—no, the fact—Arabs and Jews can be brought together in a meaningful and purposeful and redemptive way, despite all the apparati hard at work to keep them apart.

We are blessed by this fact. We are made better by this fact.

We are seeing.

The woman in her abaya and hijab doesn't really know what to do with our clapping, that stern look returned, a countenance now it seems easy to understand, given the story she has lived. But then a few smiles show up, and she nods at us, and then she and Nadia are moving toward us from the front of the room, arms out as though to herd us—it seems, on this tour, we are always being herded—and Nadia says, "Okay. Please find your seat at the tables."

We all dutifully rise from our benches, move to the tables, find seats, and now the woman in the abaya and Nadia are bringing to the table—where did they go and return from so fast?—clear glass bowls, and even as they set them down, and as I recognize what is in them, Nadia calls out to us, "Now we make *za'atar*."

And here before us are bowls of ground sumac, heaps of rich burgundy; here are bowls of golden sesame seeds, toasted and aromatic; here are Styrofoam cups of white salt; here too are bottles of olive oil; and here, here, are bowls of ground dried *za'atar the herb*, heaps the color of lavender leaves.

Hyssop, and all its concentric circles emanating out from this herb: cleansing, redemption, history and time and place.

Hope. Here in a bowl before me.

Nadia and the woman set smaller white bowls and plastic spoons in front of each of us, and Nadia instructs us on proportions, how much of each ingredient to put into our bowl, while the woman in the abaya wordlessly tends to us, nods at the color and texture of what we have made, drips in perhaps a little more olive oil from one of the bottles, spoons in just a little more sesame seed or *za'atar* or sumac.

She smiles at us now and again as she helps us.

Finally, the woman and Nadia give us each a small jar, and we spoon into them our own *za'atar the spice mixture*, screw on the lids we've been given too, and then peel off a narrow green Sindyanna label from the roll of them at the center of the table, press one end to the side of the jar, pull it snugly across the lid and then down the opposing side to seal them.

The labels are preprinted with the ingredients, a few words about the cooperative. All very neat, all very concise.

And there's the logo of this place, too, that olive tree with its profiles of two women—one Arab, we know now, the other Israeli. Together, grown and growing in the same beautiful tree.

The jars of *za'atar* are for us to keep, Nadia tells us. They are for us to take home and use on our food, so that we will remember Sindyanna, and what is happening here.

Thank you, we all say, and how wonderful this is, a real gift, a meaningful souvenir.

Both Nadia and the woman in the abaya, who is still without words, smile and nod, smile and nod.

Later, after we have lined up at the counter and made our purchases, and after we have made our long thanks and our goodbyes and thanks yet again, Or and Luke herd us out the door and down those steps and into the bus, waiting for us here at a limestone warehouse with its green bay doors, its fenced lot with metal barrels and carts and industrial-looking Other Stuff.

We file up into the bus. We take our seats.

And now, in this moment, we are quiet for the fact we have seen real peace between Arabs and Jews, peace brought about by women, and we look out our windows as the bus pulls away, this magical and mysterious tour headed on to our next destination.

An Interlude
Dining with Linda and Donald

THEY WERE a home.

Linda had written to me before we moved to Jerusalem. She was a poet—I'd read some of her work in the literary journals before she'd even contacted me—and had heard we were coming to town. She let me know she and her husband Donald were there in Jerusalem, that if we had any questions or problems or needed help to let them know and they would do all they could.

An open door, just like that.

She was an adjunct with the writing program at Bar-Ilan, and owned an art gallery in German Colony, the Jerusalem neighborhood we didn't yet know we'd be living in when she contacted us. We ended up in an apartment a five-minute walk from their home, where the art gallery was set up in the spacious foyer of their Arabic house, and featured Israeli artists whose work tended toward contemporary impressionism.

Donald was an attorney, and practiced out of their home from an office just past the gallery. Beyond that was the rest of the house: a wide dining room, rooms to left and right. Ceilings twelve feet high, light in from a house-wide bank of windows in the kitchen beyond the dining room. Outside lay the garden, with its grape vines and vegetables and flowers.

We knew all this because they invited us over for lunch one afternoon early on, and we said yes.

The house was cool inside, October still a bit warm some days, and the gallery walls, hung with their quiet and tranquil and beautiful (what other word?) images of Jerusalem streets, gave the feel of quiet and contemplation and centeredness. I have no other words, I see, as I write this.

We enjoyed being there from the start.

They hosted us on several occasions, reaching through our time living there and on to subsequent visits over the years, each time the dining room table laid with bowls and platters and plates of good food. Linda was a brilliant cook, and practiced the fine art of preparing dishes beforehand so that they were just-warm when she served them, and allowing, of course, for conversation rather than the frenetic and sweaty chaos of cooking and serving at the same time.

These meals were elegant, and they were calm, and they were riven with good conversation.

Donald was and remains the best conversationalist I have ever met. Period. He was from Providence, Rhode Island, and had gone to Harvard Law, then on to Buffalo where he met Linda, who herself had graduated from Tufts, Harvard, and then the writing program at SUNY Buffalo. Together they made *aliyah* in 1978, and had been there ever since. Five children, a number of whom, along with their spouses, we dined with on occasion, along with grandkids who brought to the table each time joy for we Americans far from home and our own loved ones.

During long afternoons bathed in sunlight in from those windows to the garden, we partook of such dishes as halibut in tomato and garlic sauce with rice, gefilte fish and spinach loaf, and Linda's tabouleh with its requisite bulgur and parsley, mint and lemon juice and olive oil, but with the added Linda-bonus of dried currants or cranberries. We had roasted chicken and roasted potatoes and roasted vegetables—cauliflower and zucchini and red peppers and sweet potatoes—and of course Israeli salad and green salad, and almonds and fresh bread and good Israeli wine.

And we talked.

Linda, soft-spoken with brown hair she wore either pulled back or in a flip that just touched her shoulders, was also a translator, and had published translations of Yehuda Amichai and Rivka Miriam, as well as two volumes of her own poetry. We talked about the literary scene in America and in Israel, the way poets and writers were so very much more valued here and not so much in the U.S.; we talked about our children, raising theirs here and ours there, and of how our older son Zeb was just then in boot camp for the Army, and the military service their children were required to observe as citizens; and we talked about food, and the freshness of ingredients to be found here, the rows of fruits and vegetables everywhere, and the fact of being searched every time you needed to go to the grocery store, the big one over on Koenig with its walled-off parking lot and security guards who looked in your trunk and glove box and purse and ran mirrors under your car to make sure you weren't bringing in a bomb before letting you pull in.

Donald, who wore a white long-sleeve dress shirt and a kippah every time we saw him, was always at ease, and gave off the air of being wise and yet humble, calm and yet engaged, smiling and even chuckling while we Americans talked about life here, and the problems of traffic on Emek Refaim, and the propensity within the culture to tell lots of Jewish jokes, of the nightly news that broadcast the ongoing saga of debates in the Knesset that threatened to shut down the government, of the quality of falafel at Doron just down the street versus the place we'd been in Bethlehem. He quizzed me on Bible stories, and one afternoon was particularly impressed I knew the origin of his Hebrew name, Gedaliah, a story in II Kings I always found particularly heartbreaking for the fact the fellow seemed a good man just doing his job to keep the peace in Judah once Nebuchadnezzar had reduced Jerusalem to rubble and hauled most everyone left to Babylon. Installed as governor by Nebuchadnezzar, he was then murdered by Ishmael, when all Gedaliah was doing was trying to take care of the beloved but destroyed nation.

Donald had nodded and smiled then, happy I'd known where his name came from. But then he'd asked in which book "By the rivers of Babylon we wept" appeared, and I, perhaps infatuated with how I'd impressed him, dropped the ball and sputtered something about maybe II Chronicles. To which Donald, smiling, wise, humble, had chuckled and said, "Nope. Psalm 137. That's about as softball a question as you're ever going to get."

I loved these conversations, when after our plates and glasses were empty and we'd pushed ourselves back from the table and rich black bitter coffee had been brought out, and we simply spent time in a home. One unlike any we'd ever known, with its gallery just inside the door, its family who weren't ours but with whom we were made to feel a part, its food just-warm and elegant and simple. Sunlight in from the windows.

It was a home we didn't know we needed while we lived so far from our own. But one we loved, and which made us feel this country and its people were perhaps a family we could, if in just the smallest way, claim as our own, we wild shoots grafted into the present vine of this land.

We were home.

The World and Beit Shemesh

LATE AFTERNOON IN July, sunflowers everywhere. Fields and fields of them, six or seven feet tall and heads high, the blooms sunflower yellow, because there is no better description to be made of that color: sunflowers are sunflower yellow.

A gang of us from the American Cultural Center has driven down from Jerusalem to Beit Shemesh, about an hour away and sort of toward Tel Aviv, to watch a minor league baseball game, these sunflower fields our company now that we're out of the Judean hills and into the farmland that stretches to the Mediterranean. We turned off Highway 1 a little while ago, where we'd passed those rusted-out military transport memorials beside the road and that Moorish caravan stop with its green trees and empty windows, before us now a sun fast on its way to setting. Beside us these fields.

We're taking a break from the planning sessions we've been in for this year's two-week teaching program. One week of planning in a meeting room at the American Cultural Center, the next week in classrooms at Be'er Sheva University in the south, where we'll teach those teachers of English from around the country three pods of American culture and literature they can bring back to their own classrooms. The planning days are long, last ten to twelve hours—this is the fourth of six days we'll spend at it—because the RELO officer, Julia, wants the program to be programmed, and as such we spend all those hours programming the programming.

We: Julia, the Regional English Language Officer; ML, the poet from Wayne State University and my partner in the whole teaching thing, we two the visiting instructors; and Jackie, the Cultural Program Specialist at the Cultural Center. Jackie's husband Derek is driving, the only one of us certain where this baseball field will be. Melanie is back home in Charleston, fresh off our having lived in Jerusalem all last fall and into January, when the visiting writer gig at Bar Ilan had ended.

39

This is the second year we've done this program together, and we all know already the days next week will be just as long. Maybe even longer, given the fact we'll all be together—students and faculty and programmers—and living on campus down south. No Mishkenot to retreat to at the end of the day, like last year.

The minor league baseball game is ML's idea, his having read somewhere about the new Israel Baseball League—this its inaugural season. Players from all over the world, minor leaguers looking to make a name ahead of being drafted—perhaps—to leagues in the States and elsewhere, all funded by an American entrepreneur. The season is into its first few weeks, with six teams and a 45 game schedule. ML has been telling us all this on the way here, and it sounds like a good idea: semi-pro baseball in a country with a high population of Americans. Many of them, that entrepreneur has gambled, looking for a little piece of America once they've made *aliyah* and settled into life in Israel.

ML is clean-shaven bald with a perfectly coiffed white goatee and moustache, the goatee long and spreading and a presence in itself, a Mormon Father's goatee that bobs extravagantly when he talks. And he talks a lot, his voice a friendly and loud and brazen growl. He also wears chunky black pointedly-hip glasses and a beret.

Poets.

"Da-ad! Are we there yet?" he calls from here in the back seat. "I don't want to miss the first pitch!" He's a funny guy, yes. But right now he's *trying* to be funny. Funny, and trying to be. Two different things.

Three of us are crammed in the back seat, me at one window, ML at the other, between us Jackie, thin and strategically seated between we two bulky writers—and we *are* bulky—to allow three of us to fit. She's smart, quick-witted, and at the end of these long days she's sometimes prickly for the pressure she's under to oversee this whole project. "Not too much further, I should think," she answers ML in her British accent, the words a little bit curt, a little bit tired.

We've all been working a lot.

Derek glances back at us from behind the wheel, smiles, says, "Nearly there," the words almost a whisper, his accent British too. He's from Newcastle, but a long time ago, having come here back in 1969, when he was just out of school. He's even thinner than Jackie, with a grizzled beard nowhere near as crisp and tenderly-wrought as ML's goatee, and wears wire-frame glasses, thin gray hair to his collar, his words always quiet, thought-out. He's a painter, with a studio in Yemen Moshe I've been to once, when we lived here and I'd cajoled him into letting me see his work. He's been painting all his adult life, has had shows all over Israel and England, but when finally I was in his studio and marveling at the work—landscapes, portraits, ethereal and full of life—and asked him why he was so reluctant to let me see his paintings, he shrugged, smiled, said as quietly and truthfully as always, "What if you didn't like it?"

I trust him. We're almost there.

"We better be close," Julia says, too loud as always, from up there on the passenger side. "I just hope there's a food truck or something. I'm starved."

She's big-boned, tall, a mop of highlighted curls atop her head. As the RELO, she's led a great deal of these educational gatherings all over the middle east. She's an American but hasn't lived there for the dozen or so years she's been with the State Department, and has an apartment in Amman, Jordan, she stays at when she's not traveling and leading sessions all over. She knows how to run things. She's used to being in charge. She's used to being blunt.

We're all already pretty tired.

Up ahead and now beside us out ML's window is a village of a sort: streets, houses, trees. A sudden appearance here in these sunflower fields, and Derek slows, pulls to the left off the road into a gravel parking area and stops. Out my window is a baseball field, and in the next moment I pop open my door, climb out.

There's a good number of cars out here, all parked at odd angles in the predictable way people here park: wedge into whatever space you can wedge into and walk away. There's a backstop past the cars, beyond that a green baseball field, the outfield fence. Beyond that rows of sunflowers.

Hills past all that, rising up and green in the not-too-distant distance. Beit Shemesh, I think. Huh.

Somewhere around here is where the Ark of the Covenant arrived back in the hands of the Hebrews, dispatched by those five Philistine kings. Their citizens riddled with tumors, their cities infested with mice, the kings wanted rid of God's presence after they'd taken the Ark as spoil from the fleeing Hebrew army. Somewhere around here two milch cows making a beeline out of Philistine territory showed up in a wheat farmer's field toting a cart with the Ark, and the people rejoiced.

A baseball field amid sunflowers, hills in the distance. A piece of the history of God somewhere right around here.

I take in a deep and solid and satisfying breath: we're taking a break.

There's what looks like a concession stand to the left on the other side of the cars, white cinderblock with a tin roof, to the right a tiny white ticket booth, a few people out front of it, and we weave between cars, get in line. Derek wants to learn all about the game, he tells us. It's been cricket his whole life, baseball this specter off in the American shadows, and immediately ML begins to tutor him, and now here we are at the booth. Twenty shekels—about six bucks—to sit in the aluminum bleachers to the left and right of the backstop, five rows and maybe twenty feet wide. Enough for a hundred people or so on either set. Or forty shekels—a little over ten bucks—to sit at the round white plastic tables with white plastic chairs directly behind the backstop and home plate.

We all look at each other, shrug. Nothing hard about this decision, and a moment later we're settling in at a table. Players are out on the field now, the home team Beit Shemesh Blue Sox in their white with blue pinstriped uniforms, their blue sox. Outfielders throw flies at each other, the infielders throwing back and forth between first base and second, first and short stop, first and third. A pitcher warms up.

The bleachers are about half full, though the game hasn't started yet, these plastic tables, maybe twenty of them, pretty much empty. There's no food truck either, though the lady at the ticket booth assured us there was one on its way down from Burgers Bar in Jerusalem, and it should be here any minute, just hold on.

Burgers Bar. Yes.

That place on Emek Refaim, maybe a five-minute walk from our apartment when we lived here, where Melanie and I went when we needed American food: a good sturdy burger; "thin fries" if you wanted them, instead of those thick British chips; onion rings. Real onion rings. The only problem with the place was that there were no cheeseburgers, dairy and meat, of course, a theo-culinary no-no for the last three thousand years.

Yes. Burgers Bar. No clue why the restaurant has that S on the end of Burger, something I always wanted to ask someone.

But onion rings. Yes.

We sit at our table, listen to ML instruct Derek in the nuances of baseball, listen to Julia talk about her apartment in Amman, listen to Jackie tell us about how, on the clearest of nights, you can actually see the lights of Amman from Jerusalem, though the city is seventy kilometers away. I go check out the concession stand—bottled water and soft drinks, popcorn, team caps and shirts—and report back to the table, where we agree to hold off on food until the Burgers Bar truck shows up.

Both teams are lined up on the baselines now, Beit Shemesh down first, the Tigers down third, their uniforms orange shirts and white pants, black socks and hats. A voice comes over loudspeakers somewhere around here, welcomes us to the game, then goes into tonight's starting lineups.

It's all very homey. All very much American. All very much, I suddenly recognize, like a high school baseball game somewhere, but maybe not even that. Maybe a community league, what with these few bleachers, these plastic tables, the field with only sunflowers past the fence.

It's a good recognition, a good moment to feel in the middle of these two weeks of work, and I listen to the lineups, expect these will all be, as with any community league anywhere, a bunch of hometown boys. They all look young, like teenagers, like kids.

But then, after the player's name, the announcer gives us the home country for each one of these Netanya Tigers, each kid stepping forward in his orange shirt and white pants and lifting his hat and waving, then stepping back into line: Japan, I hear, then a couple from Israel, the same from the U.S. Then the Dominican Republic, Canada, Colombia, Australia.

Though I know from what ML has orated inside the cramped car on the way here that this is a real live minor league, I'm still stunned they've come all the way here, to a community field, to play *baseball.*

The announcer finishes with the Netanya Tigers, then pumps up his voice a bit to introduce the home team, the fans in attendance clapping. The same thing again: though most players are from either Israel or the U.S., there's the Dominican Republic, and Australia, and Canada in there too.

Then the coach is introduced: a former player for the Yankees.

Out here. In a sunflower field.

And now that good recognition of the homeyness of this place, this right here of here, is suddenly compounded, suddenly exponentialed, suddenly utterly factual in its clichéhood, its predictability, its dim-sounding but wondrous truth: It's a small world.

Beit Shemesh and the Ark returned. Players from thousands of miles away, and right here at home. Destroyed and decaying military transports beside the roadway here. Sunflowers all facing that setting sun. American burgers and onion rings in the offing.

Good people with me. People I know for how hard we've worked together, and who care about the people they'll be helping soon enough.

The world is all right here at a community baseball field in Beit Shemesh.

More words out of the loudspeaker, me a little dazed at this all, and suddenly I'm thinking of when I was a kid following my dad to our seats at Dodger Stadium the first time—I cannot have been older than six or seven—and emerging from a concrete tunnel into the startling surprise of how huge and bright the ballfield is, the frightening fall away at my feet of steep steps down toward a green and perfect and very far away field, where tiny uniformed men play catch with each other, far to my right home plate and a miniature catcher crouched and waiting, a pitcher just as small on the mound hurling a baseball at him hard.

I'm in little league in Phoenix, and hitting the longest ball I'll ever hit, a triple, a crowd about the same size as the one gathered here cheering me on to third base.

I'm watching Fernando Valenzuela pitching the third game against the Yankees in the '81 World Series, the series where the Dodgers won four games in a row after losing the first two, Valenzuela's complete game the heart-shock they needed.

I'm a kid at a baseball game.

The words from the announcer: Please stand for the national anthem, and it seems I may be the last one up for the rush of all things through me, and here comes "Hatikvah," the tune that reminds me, the American raised American, of Topol and *Fiddler on the Roof* every time I hear it, with its minor key throughout but for the glimpses now and again of a relative major chord. Then it's back to the minor key, and all for good reason, I know: this nation's history.

But those moments of light, those bright chords nestled in there. They're there. They're history too.

And right as the black-garbed umpire calls from behind home plate "Play ball!" and just as we settle back in our seats, the bright red Burgers Bar food truck lumbers into the parking lot, settles in not thirty feet away, wedging in on this side of the cars even more boldly than any car here, inching in from the flank, inching, inching, until the driver stops, cuts the engine.

How can this get any better? There's onion rings on the way. A sturdy burger. A ball game.

But then. Then.

Because we've turned in our seats to watch this arrival happening there behind us, we can also see past the truck and past the cars a tour bus rounding in. One of the big ones, white with those sideview mirrors that reach down from the roof and to either side like giant flopped-over rabbit ears.

Plastered over the grill the canvas sign my beatific moment within this small world doesn't really want to see:

BIRTHRIGHT ISRAEL

I am not alone in my audible disappointment. All five of us at the table give a quiet groan and slowly turn back to the game, where the lead-off Tiger stands waiting for the first pitch, the pin-striped pitcher staring hard at the catcher.

Things are about to change.

Birthright buses eternally swarm the country end to end, each loaded with young American kids here on their free ten-day trip to Israel. It's a good program: If you're Jewish, age 18 to 32, and haven't lived there or stayed for more than three months, you're in for an educational tour with a posse of peers, the notion to introduce young people to the country and get them to think of their history, their religion, their culture—and the possibility of making *aliyah* yourself and moving here. Though the program doesn't like to call it a free trip to Israel—a "gift" is what they'd rather say—it's still free: airfare from particular cities across the U.S. to Tel Aviv, stays at top hotels, food, and these tours by bus. One end of the country to the other.

Everywhere. We've been there when busses have disgorged their legions of loud and happy campers at Caesarea on the coast for a run on the beach, deposited chattering droves at the Ein Gedi trailhead above the Dead Sea, and delivered them by the boisterous hundreds to Dung Gate and the way into the Western Wall, the eternal herd of buses idling away in the bus-only parking lot a little way up the hill once they've let out their loads.

One cold and bright January day while Jeff and Hart were visiting us, we were driving through the remotest of remote land in the far reaches of Ramon Crater, way down south between Be'er Sheva in the Negev and Eilat on the Red Sea, the landscape a cross between Mars and Mars. The road there was a narrow two-lane that lay across the red rock at the bottom of the craggy valley like a black shoelace, anomalous and forlorn. We'd stopped where the road crossed a wadi because Jeff, who'd since retirement as an ear, nose, and throat doctor was working toward a PhD in anthropology—he's a man with too much time on his hands—saw out his window a wide patch of grayish rock that stretched down the wash, and called out "Stop!"

Within five minutes he'd identified the spread of small flat rocks as flint, the area carpeted with nappings, and so at some prehistoric time maybe a manufacturing site for tools. Within three more minutes he'd found a flint knife, and a spearhead that seemed perhaps a castoff, one side broken away, its maker tossing it aside who knew how many eons ago.

We stood there in the cold empty valley, contemplating the passage of time, this evidence washed down from somewhere up in these cliffsides that surrounded us too many years ago to number. Whole civilizations come and gone since these implements in our hands had been created, these the only evidence of lives lived.

We were quiet. We were pondering.

And here came a tour bus from the far south of the valley, maybe a mile away. Rolling along, a rectangular white whale with those flopped-over rabbit ears, tracing its course along that shoelace, traversing this Mars, until here it was crossing the wadi, right there beside us. Across its grill the canvas sign BIRTHRIGHT ISRAEL.

The driver tooted the horn, a happy sound, cheerful and blithe—Toot! Toot!—and I thought for a moment I could see through the smoked glass windows the hands of kids waving down at us.

Then it was past, and we all watched it disappear at the other end of the valley, carefree and merry and headed somewhere else.

These buses were everywhere.

"We need to get in line at the food truck," Julia says, "before it gets mobbed."

Perhaps the wisest words passed among us the afternoon thus far, and we all make to stand. But then ML in his own wisdom suggests he and I just take orders and stand in line instead of us all, and a moment later we're headed for the truck, where one of the workers is already sliding open the window, all set to go.

We can hear the kids pouring off the bus already, next see them to the left queuing up at the ticket booth, talking, laughing. The boys all have on khaki shorts and untucked oxfords or polos, baseball caps with the bills turned back, while the girls all wear bright short shorts and linen blouses, everyone in flip flops, everyone talking.

ML and I aren't even the first in line at the truck, some of the fans here more keen than us on keeping ahead of the onslaught sure to happen, and so we take our place, and wait for the wave to hit. Then here's the crack of a bat, and all of us turn as one to see a Tiger hustling for first and rounding the base but holding up, the shot toward center dropping just past the second baseman but picked up quick by the outfielder, scaring the runner back to base.

Kids are trickling in now behind the backstop, a kind of tide picking through the plastic tables and chairs—they're all, it seems, headed for precisely where we sit—and now some of them take seats, and others tip up chairs against the tables to signal Seat Taken, and get in line behind us.

"Here we go," I say, and ML chuckles, shakes his head and with it that perfect white goatee, and we turn to the truck where it's now our turn to order.

They have no onion rings, we're informed. Only those thick British chips. It will take a while for the food too, the man tells us, so go ahead and have a seat and we'll call out your name.

I've had my moment of beautiful recognition, maybe even a borderline epiphany about this world and my place upon it. But now all that lay ahead of me is the waiting for not-onion rings, that burger those rings won't be going with. ML and I have brought back beers for all, five bottles of Goldstar, the Budweiser of Israel; next round, if there is one, will be Maccabee, the other Budweiser of Israel and the only other brand the food truck has hauled down here. The beers bring with them some semblance of the small world I'd hoped to continue enjoying—a burger, not-onion rings, and a beer. That will be okay. But there will be this swarm of kids around us, all taking their seats, all loud and pretty much oblivious to a ball game. What eighteen-year-old ever said Give me a free trip to Israel to get in touch with my heritage, religion, culture, and throw in a minor league baseball game in a sunflower field too?

But the entrepreneur of this league is pretty smart: Hook up with Birthright in the league's inaugural season and get them to buy blocks of tickets to these games. Pretty smart.

We sit. The kids fill in the tables around us, laughing, talking, laughing. They're not bad people, of course. They never are, at every place we've encountered them. Rather, they're just a knot of sound and commotion, of Messing Around. Because they're having fun. Because they're being young people among young people, and all are Jewish, and all are in Israel.

All have received a gift: this trip. But also the gift of people with a great deal in common.

And maybe because the sip of beer and its cold bitter refreshment lets me start to head back toward that small-world bliss I'd felt a little while ago, and maybe because ML, still talking of the nuances of baseball to nodding and attentive Derek, really *is* a funny guy—"I know there's a God," he says, "because of two things: seedless watermelon, and the infield fly rule"—and maybe because Julia lets out a solid laugh at that, revealing the doyen of program programming can loosen up a bit, and maybe because Jackie, the brains behind us all, the captain of the ship—the one who's organized everything from our travel here to the notebooks and pens the students will receive—looks at me with a bewildered smile, shaking her head at whatever American nonsense an infield fly rule may be, happy, it would seem, at how this break from all things has come so finely together—maybe because of all that, I'm relaxing.

It's not until the bottom of the second inning that we hear above the ground clutter of sound these kids all make around us—we've been surrounded by them, the backs of our chairs and theirs maybe a foot apart, the tables all jammed—the full-throated call "ML!" This time Derek goes with us, and we twist our way between chairs to the truck, where we finally receive our food, five foam take out trays, then balance our way back, careful upon careful not to drop these treasures. On our way we have to pass between and among and through kids whose names are likewise being called now, and finally we are back at our table, and we open up our trays, dig in.

The burger, as I'd figured and remembered, is good, and sturdy. A serious patty bedecked with sautéed mushrooms and sliced onions, a shmear of chimichurri sauce—at least the food truck had on hand the restaurant's array of sauces—all on a soft and easy-going bun. The chips are only chips, but hot, and the aroma up from it all is a quick and tangled and comforting memory of Southern California backyard barbecues and Mexican restaurants, a takeout fish and chips shop in Kilkee, Ireland where we spent a sabbatical, and autumn in the south of France, where we once lived too and foraged for fungi: there's the burger itself, the hot oil off the fries, the warm dusky earth from the mushrooms, the bright vinegar and cilantro of the chimichurri, all wrapped in the yeasty joy of this bun. The bun is even warm too.

We talk. We laugh. We start to eat.

All the kids at the table directly behind ours return with their own food, talking, laughing, and begin to eat too, and a few moments later I hear from behind me a young woman's voice say, "Excuse me."

I turn, see there in the seat closest to mine, the backs of our chairs only that foot or so away, the young woman—the kid—smiling, a chip in one hand. She sits kitty-corner to me, half turned in the chair, and wears a linen peasant blouse and bright yellow shorts, her straight black hair parted in the middle.

"You're all speaking English," she says, polite, and gives a quick nod to the others at her table, all girls, all in linen blouses, all with straight hair parted in the middle. "We were wondering where you guys are from."

"Michigan!" ML, next to me, pretty much yells out, then "Motor City!" and the kids all give a kind of cheer, burgers or chips in hand. We're all here together, all watching this minor league game, all enjoying our dinner, and so why not charge in and answer them, as ML has already done?

Julia, next to him, says, "Indiana, but I live in Jordan," to which the table gives a kind of cool-awe sound, then Derek says, "Jerusalem," the word as quiet as ever, the cool-awe sound a little quieter for it, then Jackie says, "Originally Zimbabwe, but I've been in Jerusalem for many years now." The kids, wide-eyed, nod at this exotic answer, and a couple even say "Wow," all of them smiling.

I'm in admiration of them, of their interest in others around them, and of their boldness too—at least represented by the young woman a couple feet from me who started this ball rolling.

Now it's my turn, and I say, "South Carolina."

No real cool-awe sound from anybody, just nods and smiles and chewing, and I say to them all, "Where are you guys from?"

The young woman, who isn't smiling now but looking me dead in the eye, says, "New Jersey," but quickly adds, "You're from South Carolina?"

"Yep," I say and nod, look to the young woman beside her, who has blonde hair and touches at her mouth with a napkin in preparation for her answer. But the one beside me says, "Where in South Carolina?"

I smile, look at her. She's holding her burger now, has it half-way up. But she's stopped, waiting for me before she can take a bite.

"Charleston," I say, and look at the girl next to her again.

But the one who started this all says, "What do you do?" and sets her hamburger back in her tray.

I glance back to my own table, see all these good people looking first at me, then the girl, me, the girl. They're wondering what this is all about.

I turn back to her. "We're here to teach a kind of conference. But I'm a professor."

"Where?" she shoots back, her hands now in her lap, holding a napkin.

I give a quick glance to my table again. I don't want all this attention. I don't like people looking at me. There are other people here, can't she see? Other more interesting people than me. Derek here, he's an artist! Jackie's family got kicked out of Rhodesia! Look at ML, a poet wearing a beret! Look at that goatee! Motor City! And Julia. Julia. She has a new perm, and she's in charge!

But I just turn back to her, say, "The College of Charleston."

"What's your name?" Quick as that.

And I have no choice but to answer her. "Bret Lott," I say.

Her mouth opens wide, her eyes too, and she takes in a breath, says in one long word too loud, too loud, "I'm-trying-to-get-into-your-creative-writing-course-but-it's-full-can-you-give-me-an-override?"

There.

The world is, I feel and know and believe and am certain, finally and after all and as it turns out, *too* small. Way too small.

Astonished laughs across the table, her friends nodding, leaning back from the table in a kind of crazy awe, mouths full of burgers and fries, and I hear the same kind of laughter behind me at my own table, these turncoats who don't quite realize this means I am no longer simply enjoying the being of being here—the anonymity of being present and witnessing the world at Beit Shemesh—but have now been spotted in it.

Pinned to it, in a way. A moth a moment ago bouncing around the candle of now, now with a needle through it and affixed to a foam board.

It was fun while it lasted.

Yet everyone laughs, everyone with "How cool!" and "What a small world!" and "This is crazy!" Lots and lots of cool-awe sounds.

I'm smiling, slowly shaking my head, and say, "You came all this way just to try and get into my class?" and people laugh again.

But I don't want to think right now about work back home. I want to be here. I want to be, simply put, left alone.

The girl says, "No! Really! Can I get in?" She has her hands in front of her, seems almost to bounce in her seat.

And I see now what it means to be in a small world: There is no being left alone. It's a small world precisely because you are one of those upon it, and a part of it too.

"You got me cornered," I say, then, "Yes. What else am I going to say, all the way out here in Israel?"

And already I'm coming around, allowing in a kind of cool-awe of my own, and I shake my head and smile back at my colleagues—my friends—and at this student, and the colleagues of hers gathered at the table.

A really small world.

The Blue Sox will win the game. They'll go on to win the championship too, defeating the Modi'in Miracle in August. And this will be the Israel Baseball League's one and only season, turnout to the games just not enough to make any money.

The student—Jenna is her name—will show up in my class that fall, and prove herself, though only a brand-new freshman in an upper division course, to be a fine writer, a tough critic, and sometimes too talkative to let others into the conversation. She'll settle down after a while, then graduate and move back to New Jersey. But that first day in class when I call out her name, we'll both tell the story of how she got into this closed course, and yet again there will come cool-awe sounds and laughter.

After the game and before we head back to Jerusalem, I'll buy a Blue Sox baseball cap at the concession stand, black with a white team logo, the Hebrew initials for Beit Shemesh. I'll wear it when I mow my lawn, people in my neighborhood wondering what the heck that logo means, me with my very own little secret.

Once we're all back in the car, night full on us and Derek leading us out from this village with its trees and houses and streets, I'll say out loud, "Beit Shemesh. There's so much history here," thinking on that cart, those cows, the golden Ark returned.

"Oh," Derek will say, and look back at me, his face a dull green for the dim light off the dashboard. "This isn't Beit Shemesh. This is Kibbutz Gezer. Beit Shemesh is another 30 kilometers to the south. They play here because this is the only baseball field anywhere around."

And I'll feel a bit of disappointment at the news.

But right now we're only into early evening, this summer afternoon coming to a close, those sunflower yellow sunflowers out past the ballfield fence all lolled to one side. Another day in the history of the world almost done.

Who would have thought.

What to Drink: Café Hafuch

THE APARTMENT WE HAD while we lived there was a small one: a front room with a dining area, kitchen, a bedroom, a bathroom. A loft-type thing up a steep set of stairs, more a ladder than anything else, to a space you had to crawl in on hands and knees were you to sleep on the futon wedged up there. The whole was what people kept calling an Arab apartment, though I could never nail down exactly what that meant. Tall ceilings, bronzed ironwork window frames, an elaborate Moorish sort of round-topped front door of opaque glass and that iron. All in limestone.

But small.

So I took to writing in a place called Café Hillel, right across Emek Refaim from the apartment. From our front steps you could see its black awning above glass walls, the place no bigger than a Pizza Hut. A lighted red sign with white letters in Hebrew and English both on the wall out front, on it the black silhouette of what looked like a businessman—hat, overcoat, cuffed pants—in purposeful, almost jaunty midstride. Though I'd never written in a café before, I wanted to give it a try. The apartment was so small there was no place to be alone, and Melanie and I had been married long enough to know that to spend every single waking moment together was not a very good way to spend every single waking moment.

And there was a novel to get written, already a year late.

They opened at 6:45, and I made it my mission, purposefully, almost jauntily, to be the first one in the door each morning. Usually I succeeded, the nonplussed employee all in black at the glass door with her keys turning the lock never making eye contact. But that didn't matter. I had a novel to write.

The first few days I ordered the timidly predictable: café Americano. Espresso with hot water poured in. But once I told my class at Bar-Ilan about my writing routine now that I was here, they all shouted in what seemed one voice, Try a *café hafuch*.

They also told me that particular Café Hillel—it was a small chain with locations across the country—had been the site of a suicide bombing three years before. Seven people killed, plus the bomber. Among the dead had been a doctor and his daughter, who was to have gotten married the next day.

Hadn't I seen the plaque out front, there beneath the sign?

No, I'd told them.

And now I was worried, selfishly, about my safety. Was it all right to go there? I asked them. Would I be safe?

To which they all sort of let out deep sighs, smirked, slowly shook their heads at the ignorance of this guy who was supposed to be the wise teacher: Of course you're safe. They never bomb a place twice. You're safer at that branch than any other one in the country.

And get a *hafuch*.

The next morning, waiting outside for the no-eye-contact barista, I stood back from the front door, and looked at the red sign, and the plaque beneath it. Yes, I realized only then, I had in fact seen this before, a simple stone plaque the same beige as the Jerusalem stone wall it was attached to. Maybe two feet tall and a foot and half wide. *Humble* was the word that came to me, and then *quiet*. The words were all in Hebrew, the only color to the memorial a stylized red flame, as if from a lit candle, at the top.

A memorial I hadn't known was a memorial, me a foreigner here, I was reminded, unaware yet again and always of the battle always going on.

Café hafuch: upside-down coffee. Upside down because instead of pouring hot milk into espresso as you would with a cappuccino, hot milk goes in first, the espresso poured in next—carefully, slowly, so that it doesn't yet mix with the milk, making a very nifty two-tone drink. Milk froth goes on top. It's served in a glass, or at least was at Café Hillel, with the end result striated layers top to bottom: white froth on the top, next the deep brown espresso, then the bottom hot milk, gone a little tan for the espresso poured on top of it.

And, strangely, oddly, it's better than a cappuccino.

I learned also to order it *godal vay hazack*, large and strong, and suddenly, after maybe the third week of showing up first thing each morning outside the store with my computer bag in hand to meet the barista-who-would-not-make-eye-contact, then stepping boldly to the counter and ordering up my *café hafuch godal vay hazack*, I felt somehow like I was becoming a regular. Someone who might live around here. Someone who maybe belonged.

Yet by the time I needed a second one each morning the place was filled with people who really belonged, Sabras and transplants alike, all jammed up at the counter and ordering their coffees, cutting in front of each other and cutting again, all of it as chaotic as always. Every man and woman for themselves. Same as ever.

Then I'd ruefully, timidly commit to making my way over and take my own place, eventually ordering *café hafuch* large and strong, while back at the table a novel waited, and waited, and waited to get written.

One morning before that second cup a couple came in and sat down at the table next to mine, a man and woman a little older than me, sharply dressed (I always wore my writing uniform: a pair of jeans and my trusty old blue Eddie Bauer sweatshirt) in tweed jackets and turtleneck sweaters, hers white, his gray, both with short and spiky white hair, cut and styled, it was hard not to imagine otherwise, by the same hand. Before them sat their *hafuchs* layered just so.

They were speaking Hebrew—no surprise—but so loudly that I could hear them through my earphones, a cool noise-reducing set I'd gotten for Father's Day, music an integral part of this whole writing thing. I can't write unless I'm listening to music I've decided upon for its resonance, tone, amicable partnership with the thing I'm trying to make. This novel, it turned out, was set to Bill Frissell's *The Willies*, but now the spooky atmospherics of the banjo and electric and acoustic guitars, the slightly askew backdrop loops and lonesome bass, all peeled away.

A loud couple sat beside me.

So I was a bit annoyed, me trying to work, and afraid to turn up the volume too high because I didn't want to go deaf too quickly. And then, maybe to give the woman the side-eye so she could see I was bothered, maybe to give a small shake of the head to signal them both they were being so very loud, and couldn't they see someone beside them trying to do something here?—right then I looked up from the computer to their table.

But the woman had stopped talking. She was sitting up straighter now than I'd noticed before, her short gray hair, it seemed, almost at attention too, her back not touching the banquette that ran along the back wall where we were seated. Then suddenly—the word doesn't render the quick surprise of her movement—she stood, ran through the café, around all these tables loaded with the morning crowd, and to that glass front door, where I could see now a child—a toddler maybe three—standing with a stuffed animal of some sort caught in the closed door, the doll half inside and half out.

Her mother, pushing a stroller in front of her and just inside the café, hadn't seen her daughter behind her as the door had closed, and before she'd even noticed, could even turn around to see, the woman beside me— the loud woman, the annoying woman—had made it to the child, pushed open the door, and freed the stuffed animal.

The woman smiled down at the girl, and her mother turned around at the commotion, surprise on her face: eyebrows up, mouth open. Her eyes went from her child to the woman to her child, and the woman said something, smiling, and then the mother smiled, nodded, and the child looked up at them both as though they were strangers, the stuffed animal tight in her arms.

The woman returned to the table, where she sat down, and took a sip of her *hafuch*, and she and her husband started talking again, as though nothing happened.

I waited, watched the mother with the stroller and little girl, expecting them to come to join the two at the table beside me. Maybe they were family, the mother the woman's daughter, for how intimate the help had been from all the way across the restaurant.

But nothing happened, except that the mother went up and ordered, then pushed the stroller to a table for herself and her children, the toddler and her animal trailing only a foot or so behind, the mother with her eye on her now and again as they made their way through the room, then sat.

All that way she'd carried her own *hafuch*, the glass cup settled on its saucer, the layers delicate and purposeful.

Soon I'd have to go get my second *café hafuch*. But for now I did nothing, only paused the music, slipped off the headphones, and sat there, listening. Not just to the two beside me, but to all the noise around me, all this hubbub. All these people.

All this life.

Security

THE FRONT PASSENGER door on the silver Suburban weighs what feels a good three hundred pounds, and I have to pull with both hands to open it. The vehicle is armored and has bulletproof glass, Akeem told me on the way over from Mishkenot Sha'ananim, where Melanie and I are staying yet again.

Now I am at the curb out front of the American Consulate on Agron Street, with its squared-stone wall and wide sidewalk and security stands and guards in blue shirts with ID cards on lanyards around their necks. The stone wall is topped with razor wire, on the other side the complex of stone buildings and the three story consulate itself, the grounds lush with palms and cypress and pine trees and roses.

But right now there is only the business of this Suburban passenger door, and how heavy it is, until finally I have it open.

"Shotgun!" I say, and climb in, the word out of me too loud for the small joke it is.

The driver, already seated behind the wheel, laughs, and Akeem and Maryam laugh too, the two of them climbing into the back seat. Akeem: director of the America House, a cultural engagement center and part of the American Consulate, and a Federal agent; Maryam: American Consulate Cultural Programs Specialist. Melanie isn't allowed on today's trip, though she was with us the whole day yesterday. But that was in Bethlehem and East Jerusalem. Technically the West Bank, yes, but safe enough to allow a kind of spousal dispensation for her from the consulate.

There will be no dispensation today. Today we're going to Ramallah.

I pull the door closed, then turn to the driver. "I'm Bret," I say, and he nods, says, "I know." He's still smiling for the bad pun about riding shotgun into the West Bank. "I am Moshe," he says, and we shake hands. He's young, a national with a thick accent, aviator sunglasses and black spiky hair. A little like Zoolander. He lets go my hand, then takes the radio mic from the console. "Moshe to Houston," he says into the mic. "Leaving Post 1."

"Roger," a voice comes back on the radio. A very American voice, a southern voice, I can hear on just that one word.

Houston, I think, and smile. Mission control.

Then we pull away from the curb into morning Jerusalem traffic. Just ahead of us down the four lane street is the massive white limestone Mamilla Hotel and the outdoor mall, a wide pedestrian boulevard lined with Ralph Lauren and Gucci and Gap stores, cafes and galleries, all of it in that limestone, all of it beautiful and new. Beyond it all, at the top of Mamilla, stands Jaffa Gate and the high walls of old Jerusalem itself, the limestone there leached and weathered. Older every time we come here and see it.

Ramallah is, were a straight line possible, eight miles away. But the Consulate General's Program Schedule for the three days I am here to speak on being a writer has allotted an hour to get there, because there is no straight line.

There is a wall around which we must travel. Yet even that word—wall—is a political statement, I know. In Israel, it's known as the Separation Barrier. Or the Security Fence. But, well, the fact is, it's a wall.

Akeem leans forward between the seats, says, "We'll be safe today. There's an advance team in front of us, probably a half mile or so, just to make sure everything's clear. They'll be with us all day. And there's an extraction team in Ramallah."

I turn to him, there in his blue suit and black tie, white dress shirt. Before I'd met him yesterday I'd only known him through emails, and figured a guy named Akeem must be from this part of the world. But he's an American through and through, born in Greenville, South Carolina, his southern accent almost nonexistent but there, just there. Thirty-something and tall, black hair and olive skin, he was for years an Army Ranger until he stepped into the State Department and the Consulate here in Jerusalem, his wife working in the embassy in Tel Aviv. Just past him sits Maryam, in her twenties with long black hair and porcelain skin. Born and raised in Bethlehem, her English is excellent though sometimes a little laden with her Arabic accent. She's got on a black pantsuit, a green silk blouse. She nods at me, and this good news from Akeem: there's an extraction team in Ramallah.

"An extraction team?" I say. "Really?"

"We're perfectly safe," Akeem says, and smiles, gives a nod and eases back in the seat. "But we have to be careful."

"There is no worry," Maryam says.

But here's the thing: here's the thing: I'm not worried. All of this is fun. I'm learning something, going somewhere I've never been.

I am a writer, going to talk to people about writing.

Still. An extraction team.

The driver, who is, of course, security, says something into the mic I don't catch for his accent.

"Copy," comes back from mission control, then, "Proceed."

This is our fifth visit to Israel. For the first half of the trip I've been a guest of Bar-Ilan University, my old employer in Tel Aviv, as part of their seventh anniversary celebration of The Shaindy Rudoff Graduate Program in Creative Writing. Shaindy, a writer with a vision to bring creative writing in English to Israel, was the one, during my first trip here, who asked if I would think about coming to teach at Bar-Ilan for a semester and serve as writer-in-residence. We were at a cocktail party put on by someone in the American Consulate at an apartment in the limestone Mamilla complex, where all those tony stores are lined up now. But then, eight years ago, the mall was only under construction, the street and its windowless storefronts a kind of wind tunnel shuttling the late evening breeze up toward Jaffa Gate when the group of us from the American Center approached the building.

The apartment—modern, relaxed, limestone—was filled with hobnobbers hobnobbing, and because I am at core a very shy person, I was, as ever, ill at ease, trying to make small talk with all these impressive people. Then a young woman came up to me and introduced herself—Shaindy Rudoff, from Bar-Ilan University—and broke the accumulated ice I'd been collecting since my arrival. She was from New York, a writer and teacher, and helped edit *Maggid*, the literary journal published here. She was sharp, and funny, and on a kind of mission: She let me know she was the founder and director of the graduate creative writing program, and then and there asked if I would think about applying for a Fulbright Senior American Scholar position to teach at the university the next year. She'd read a couple of my books, knew *The Southern Review*, and wanted to know would I be willing to spend a semester here.

Just like that.

At the end of that first trip here and its two weeks teaching in the State Department's English language and culture program for Israeli teachers from around the country, Melanie arrived and we spent one more week visiting tourist spots: the Holy Sepulcher, the Western Wall, the Temple Mount and the Dome of the Rock, then out to Qumran and the caves where the Dead Sea Scrolls were found, and to the Dead Sea itself.

And I decided to take up Shaindy's offer. We'd move here.

All spring that next year, I stayed in touch with Shaindy. She set up my teaching schedule for the fall, ordered books for the class, sent contact info for other professors and writers, even helped us find a place to live. We spoke in late May of 2006 about exactly that, how one of the grad students owned an apartment in German Colony right on Emek Refaim, the main drag through the colony and only a few minutes' walk to the gardens that overlooked the Old City—the perfect location for living in Jerusalem.

Then, in mid-June, I received a phone call from the Department of English telling me that Shaindy had passed away.

This didn't make sense—I'd just spoken with her about where we might live; I'd been in touch all spring; she was young; she was sharp, and funny.

She'd been fighting cancer for a good many years, I was told. Many years. She'd last spoken to me from her hospital bed, where she'd given me the lead on the perfect apartment in German Colony.

She didn't want to bother people with the matter, I was told. She wanted to make sure this program in writing wasn't distracted by her sickness. She wanted to ensure people who wanted to write in English in Israel would have the opportunity. She wanted the imagination to be practiced, and to be celebrated.

She was forty.

Then the program was named after her in honor of that vision, and that desire, and in the evenings when the desert air had begun to cool, Melanie and I walked from that apartment up Emek Refaim to Yemen Moshe and the terraced beds of lavender and stone at Bloomfield Garden, the Old City only a couple hundred yards east across the Hinnom Valley. A place where, when the air was clear enough, we could see the pale blue skin of the Dead Sea fifteen miles away and nearly 4,000 feet below us, past that the mountains of Moab in Jordan.

For the past five days—eight years after meeting her, seven since living here—we've been here to celebrate her, and the program. I've attended a commemorative gathering—a cocktail party, actually—in perhaps the same apartment as where I met Shaindy there in Mamilla all those years ago, and listened to reminiscences about her; I met her mother at the party, told her of what a fine daughter she had, a visionary, then was asked, as a past writer-in-residence, to say a few words about her. I told the story of her helping secure our apartment and those cool evenings, and the fact I never knew a thing while she worked to accommodate Melanie and me. The few and impromptu words out of me surprised me with my recognizing the depth of that commitment, that vision, her calling me from a hospital bed that last time, and then my chin had betrayed me and revealed that sudden depth I hadn't known I was wading into, and I had to stop, and thank her mother, and simply go quiet.

At Bar-Ilan, I've led a workshop in writing the memoir, given a reading, been interviewed by the writer Joan Leegant on stage, where the power went out twice, the entire auditorium gone black. The first time lasted only a minute or so, but the second time the place stayed dark, and so Joan, a former grad student of mine at the Vermont College MFA program and now a wonderfully well-published writer teaching in the program at Bar-Ilan, pulled out her cell phone, turned on the flashlight, and went right ahead with the interview. I turned mine on too, and we went like that for another half-hour, questions and answers back and forth, our faces illuminated like kids at a campfire holding flashlights beneath our chins, telling tales of writing and rejection and tenacity, and why it's the story that matters, and why words matter, and imagination matters, because who are we without the *story*, and the words to give it?

I've also taught a day-long—very long—seminar on writing the novel in the apartment we'd been given for our stay, twelve people crowded into the living room of a beautiful two-story place in Yemen Moshe owned by Bar-Ilan. A long day, but made enjoyable not only by the eagerness of those gathered, all embarked upon their own writing lives, but also the view from its back patio onto the Old City even closer than at Mishkenot, only a couple hundred yards to our right along the limestone alleyways of this enclave. On our breaks throughout the day we stepped outside onto the patio, talked of books and the tenacity it takes to write one, the hope, and the gamble, while around us lay Yemen Moshe, the sort of Beverly-Hills-meets-Soho of Jerusalem. Narrow limestone streets terrace down the hill from up at Montefiore Windmill to the floor of the Hinnom, the alleyways lined with apartments with flourishing gardens behind low limestone walls, most every house with a view to the Old City. All of it pedestrian only, all of it intimate, all of it quiet and historic and beautiful. Geraniums and bougainvillea in full bloom everywhere, crowding in from planters and windowboxes and hanging baskets all along the narrow streets, exploding in orange and red and purple.

Once those five days with Bar-Ilan were over, Melanie and I packed up and wheeled our rolling duffels along the alleyways across to Mishkenot, where we checked in for part two of this visit, a series of readings and discussions on writing in the West Bank and East Jerusalem, sponsored by the State Department.

Invited here by Michael Richards, Public Affairs Officer with the American Consulate and my school chum from thirty years before, when we were students together in the MFA program at UMass Amherst. Back from his latest post in South Korea. Michael, who'd invited me originally all the way back in 2003, ten years ago now.

We met at Mishkenot yesterday morning when he and the driver came to pick Melanie and me up. He was older—of course!—and had shaved his head, and had on a light green suit and blue shirt and tie. Last time I'd seen him all any of us ever wore were jeans and T-shirts, and we both had a lot more hair.

But here he was, the same old Michael: slightly cynical, quick-witted, gregarious and, like me, like us all, older.

We'd headed to East Jerusalem and the America House, inside the walled compound to the north of Damascus Gate—a tranquil garden of roses and olive trees, palms and grass and chairs and tables on limestone patios. The house itself was an older two story home where the consulate held movie nights and conversational English classes and hosted lectures, all for nationals living in East Jerusalem and the West Bank, and where a reporter from *Al Quds*, the daily Arabic-language newspaper, met me for an interview. *Why are you here?* he asked, a very good question that made me think, and then answer with *Because I love this place, and these people, and I want to share with them what I think I may know about how to write your own story.*

It seemed a good answer, at least to me, and true. It seemed as well to please the reporter, who smiled, nodded, wrote down the words.

Then we'd left for our first stop, Bethlehem University, where I'd be giving a talk to students on writing. The black Suburban we were in yesterday, Shmuel of the airport runs our driver, headed south out of Jerusalem and then effortlessly through the security checkpoint at the twenty-five-foot wall—the Separation Barrier, the Security Fence—that borders Bethlehem, and then on up Hebron Road to the university.

Inside its limestone walls lay a landscaped campus filled with cedars and pine, terraces of rosemary and lavender beds, roses everywhere. Students, mostly women in their stylish silk hijabs, walked between buildings headed to classes, talking, laughing, on cell phones, sitting on benches in the shade of those cedars and pine.

Much like any campus anywhere. Students laughing, talking.

Safe.

Now Moshe leads us north out of Jerusalem city traffic to the French Hill area, hillsides carpeted with homes and apartments, then off to the east and through the security checkpoint on the highway that leads down to the Dead Sea. There's no wall here, only concrete road barriers on either side of the highway as it narrows down to the booths at the checkpoint itself. Wire fences and razor wire extend perpendicular to either side of the roadway, and a soldier steps out of the booth as we approach, five or six other soldiers here and there, watching traffic. They all seem only boys and girls, high school students dressed up as though in costume in their standard issue light green fatigues, light green berets, assault rifles strapped on. But the women—can I say girls?—have long hair either pulled back in pony tails or loose; one or two of the boys smoke cigarettes and they all wear kippahs.

The soldier out of the booth talks to Moshe, who shows him his ID. The soldier stares at it a long few seconds, then looks inside the vehicle, at me, at Akeem and Maryam, then one more time at me. Then he nods to Moshe, and we pull away, off into the desert, these hills.

"This is going to take a little longer," Akeem says, and I turn, look over my shoulder to see him leaned forward. "But we won't have to go through the Separation Barrier this way. Just a lot easier."

He's not worried at all, this former Ranger. He's got confidence. And I'm still having fun, because we're driving in the West Bank, and isn't it a very interesting thing, having an extraction team out there somewhere that knows exactly where we are?

What we drive through is, simply, desert. Not much different—my touchstone always—than Southern California, this time the desert out past Indio on the I-10 toward Arizona. Hills and scrub and highway.

But there's life out here. We pass Israeli settlements now and again, tidy upheavals of homes and buildings perched atop hills and fenced all the way around. We pass Arab villages too, the same sort of hilltop gatherings, but these houses and buildings unfenced, the upper stories of so many of them unfinished. Rebar sticks up from the flat roofs, second- and third-story walls with glassless windows and no roofs on many others. Olive groves are out there too, low stone walls in long lines that square off rocky fields where gray-green trees rise up despite the brown dead grass everywhere.

There's a low-lying tent city we pass, too, this off the side of a hill, out of the wind. A Bedouin community, clusters of tarps and blankets and whatever can be found held up with ropes and what seem ancient tree limbs and two by fours. A few beat-up cars and trucks sit in the dirt around the tents, and plastic chairs, barrels, old sofas, cardboard boxes. Debris is the word that comes to me.

Then here, out the window, is a bright and shiny grocery store complex, two stories, a parking lot filled with cars, bright green letters like a marquee announcing the store's name. It's new, Akeem tells me when I ask, a place built for the Israelis living in their settlements out here.

I'm in the West Bank.

We'd leased a car for the five months we lived here, and drove from one end of the country to the other: Eilat on the Red Sea in the south, Tiberias and Migdal and Capernaum in the Galilee, Be'er Sheva and Tel-Megiddo and Caesarea, Ramon Crater in the Negev and Belvoir Castle in the Jordan River Valley, the Crusader fortress high on a rocky bluff looking down on the green river.

We saw all this, and more. But there were places we weren't allowed to go.

When we'd arrived that September, we'd had a mandatory meeting with the State Department's Fulbright liaison in Israel. "You are not allowed into the West Bank while you're here," he'd told us point blank there in his office in a Tel Aviv high-rise. Out the windows behind his desk we could see the Mediterranean, the azure blue of the water, the wide white band of the beach. "Were something to happen to you, we might not have the assets available to extract you. You'd be on your own. So you are not allowed in to the West Bank."

Afterward, Melanie and I commented on the view from his office, that blue and the white. We'd debated for a moment going to the beach and taking a walk, but put it off, deciding we'd do that another time. We'd both grown up in Southern California, the beach a part of life, always there. Here we wanted Antiquity, we wanted History. We wanted to see what we could never find back home.

And of course we wanted in to see the West Bank. But we only made it as far in as Bethlehem, and that only twice. The first time, we were brought there by a friend—a Baptist missionary—who'd lived in Israel for ten years and owned a car with Israeli plates, and so we'd be allowed to drive through the security checkpoint and that twenty-five-foot wall into Bethlehem with no more than glances at our passports.

On the Israeli side of the wall and to the right of the entry portal—a narrow two-lane street that passed through the wall—was strapped a giant square tarpaulin sign that stretched from the top of the wall to the bottom. At the top of the sign were three huge colored squares in a row—magenta, green and orange—inside each the stylized Ministry of Tourism logo of two people, more bathroom icons than anything else, facing in one direction and carrying between them a pole on their shoulders, on each pole a different symbol: a palm tree on the first, a camera on the second, a sunrise on the third. We'd seen the logo all over the country indicating tourist points of interest, but usually on the pole between the two figures hung a stylized bunch of giant grapes, a reference to the Biblical spies in Numbers who scout out the land and find it flowing with milk and honey, bringing back as proof a cluster of grapes so big two of them have to carry it between them on a pole. Every time I'd seen the logo it occurred to me there might have been a piece of unexamined irony to the Ministry of Tourism's using it, as these were the same spies who, save for Joshua and Caleb, said the Promised Land couldn't be taken for the size and number of its inhabitants. Their report, and its effects on the already-grumbling chosen people, made for a forty-year side trip during which no one partook of anything. Or visited any tourist spot.

But here were these logos all the same, huge up there at the top of the wall in their colored squares. Beneath them were three more colored bands that ran the width of the sign, in each one letters just as big as the icons. "Peace Be With You" read the first, below that Hebrew words for, I could only guess, the same blessing, and beneath that the same in Arabic. All bright, all cheerful. All very Ministry of Tourism.

We drove through the portal then, and were officially in Bethlehem. The West Bank, where we weren't allowed to go.

But we were with our American friend who had lived here for ten years. We'd be safe in Bethlehem, he'd told us. Nothing would happen, and if something did, he'd be there to take care of us.

Turned out he knew people everywhere in town, from the proprietor of a shawarma and falafel shop that remains to this day the best place I have ever eaten both, to the archbishop of the Armenian Orthodox contingency that shares, with the Roman Catholic and Greek Orthodox, the care of the Church of the Nativity and the Grotto itself. The archbishop just happened to be out in Manger Square when we arrived, and we'd posed for pictures with him in front of the Door of Humility, the four-foot-tall stone entranceway to the sanctuary. The holy man, there in his dark red robe and white beard, scowled for the camera, though just before and as soon as the pictures were taken he was a smiling and friendly and gentle man.

And our friend knew too the owners of the oldest olive wood workshop in Bethlehem. We followed him onto a side street off Manger Square into a stone building with a green metal awning, above it a large white sign with the words OLD CAVE SOUVENIR and a list of what one might find inside: ALL KINDS OF GIFTS JEWELLERY OLD ICONS OLIVE WOOD MOTHER OF PEARL OLD DRESSES.

The front door of the place was the same green as the awning, and stood open, hanging from it two traditional dresses, long and black and embroidered at the cuffs and neck and bodice in bright patterns. Inside was filled with too many nativity scenes to number, and we'd sat huddled within them all and visited with the family—the mother, her two sons, a couple grandchildren. Next we'd been shown the workshop itself in a cave beneath the store, where yet another grandson sent up a shower of sawdust as he shaped wood at a lathe. Back in the shop we'd been brought fresh coffee, thick as syrup and bittersweet, the tiny handleless cups served on a silver tray. The family had treated us as tradition would have it: with grace and generosity, never pressuring us to buy anything, only expressing gratitude at having visitors, what with how difficult the economy had turned, now that the wall had been built.

The older son, tall and maybe forty and with excellent English, had known our friend for most of the ten years he'd lived in Israel, and told us that any time we were visiting we would have to stop in again.

We bought an olive wood nativity scene, and thanked them for their hospitality, and the coffee, and the good heart they'd shown us, then drove on back to the wall, and to Jerusalem, astonished at the nonsense of a State Department liaison's warnings of extraction and assets.

The highway through the desert hugs the sides of these rocky hills, and we pass a green road sign that reads in three languages—Hebrew first, Arabic next, then English—3 Bet El, 4 Ramallah. We're almost there.

Akeem leans forward again from the backseat, gives more info on who we'll meet and what we'll do this morning in Ramallah. We'll be visiting with the director of a non-profit Palestinian NGO that provides children and young people a place and resources for reading and writing and the arts, the group primarily a publisher of children's books and which serves as a literary hub in the West Bank. They sponsor reading circles, workshops for young writers, book publication launches. A very successful group providing kids with opportunities to read, and to write, and to grow to love books.

"Sounds great," I say, then add, "But you know I haven't written any children's books." Out the window now the desert slowly gives way to more buildings, square, limestone. Shops: car parts, a small grocery store, what seems maybe a laundromat for the piles of clothing in carts out front. But it's all still desert.

"That's okay," Akeem says, that ghost of a South Carolina accent on his words. "This is just to meet people. The important thing is connection. We're not expecting anything other than to meet."

"She is a wonderful lady," quiet Maryam says then, and I look back at her, see she's smiling, but not in some sort of pasted-on way. She's happy, I can see, that we are going to this place. "You will enjoy meeting the director," she says. "This group is doing very good work for its people." She goes on to tell me of how four years ago the center received an extraordinary international award for its work in Gaza and the West Bank helping young people read, and nurturing their imagination.

We've been together for two full days now, and these are the most words I've heard from her.

She nods then, and the matter, it feels to me, is settled. We are going to see good people doing good things, and I believe her.

The highway rises up a hillside, fields out past the now-and-again buildings, until now, as we curve to the right around one more low hill, I can see a traffic circle ahead, at its center a concrete spire that looks for all the world like an upside-down golf tee a hundred feet tall, and suddenly off to the left is a city, a sudden appearance: high-rises, low buildings, billboards. We round the traffic circle, pass on the right first an empty lot, then a gas station, next a hotel six or seven stories high, and then we exit the roundabout onto a wide boulevard, a median down its middle landscaped with palm trees.

A city.

Apartment buildings everywhere. People walking. Restaurants, more stores, and now a Dodge and Jeep dealership. Those billboards advertise telephone companies and restaurants, movies and clothing. Wide sidewalks line either side of the boulevard, all landscaped, and glass and limestone hotels rise up impressively beside us, traffic all around, trucks and cabs and motorcycles and bikes.

People.

We slow to a light, and I look past Moshe, our security, and see out his window a Starbucks with its round green and white logo, smoked-glass windows, a slope of ground out front covered with astroturf. It's on the ground floor of a high-rise, and I give a small laugh, think, Even Ramallah has a Starbucks, and for a moment I want to ask if we can go in there, see if they have Ramallah Starbucks travel mugs like they sell in big cities: a souvenir coup.

Then I look again at the logo, and what I have become inured to—that green and white round sign with the mermaid in the middle isn't the Starbucks logo at all. "Stars & Bucks," the logo reads on the top of the circle, at the bottom "Café." And instead of the green and white mermaid in the center there are the brims of four steaming cups of coffee.

"Hah!" I let out. "Look at that!" I say, all in a kind of oddball glee.

Moshe glances out the window, lets out a short breath through his teeth, slowly shakes his head.

Akeem says from behind me, "I'm betting Starbucks isn't going to sue them any time soon," and Maryam gives a small laugh.

The strange thing, though, about seeing that logo and the store in the moments before it becomes a rather clever and litigious-free West Bank coffee shop is that I feel for some reason somehow a little bit safer.

Here seems a small piece of home.

Melanie and I like Starbucks, have been going there since the mid-80s when we discovered this new place one afternoon in Laguna Beach, there at the pavilion on Pacific Coast Highway, right downtown. This new thing: a shop selling fine hot drinks, named after the good man who served as first mate on Ahab's *Pequod*.

We'd sat on the beach across the street from that Starbucks with our friends Dave and Lora, and watched our two little boys, Zeb and Jake, mess around in the sand, and drank our coffees. A beautiful afternoon.

So, maybe, in discovering that moment of apparent safety—a Starbucks! Just like home!—I've also discovered that, well, perhaps I might not be feeling as safe as I may seem. Maybe I'm not as *not* worried as I believe, going to this somewhere I've never been.

The second time we went to Bethlehem the year we were told not to go was in December, a month or so after that first visit with the friend who drove us in. Our son Jacob had come to spend his winter break with us—he was a junior at the College of Charleston—and at the same time my mother came out from Seattle to spend Christmas with us. My father had passed away in July that year, and Melanie and I thought a visit to the Holy Land—a lifelong dream of my mother's—might be of some help as she began to move through her life without her husband of fifty-one years. And so, emboldened with the success of that first time in to Bethlehem, Melanie and I, the seasoned travelers in Israel we'd become, decided we'd bring them in ourselves. Who needed guides, or a tour bus? We'd been there. A friend with the right license plates? We knew our way around.

We parked the leased car in the parking lot on the Israel side of the wall—no rentals are allowed into the West Bank—then stopped at the wall and took pictures of Jacob in front of that massive and colorful sign wishing us peace in three languages. It was a cold morning, Melanie and my mother and I all dressed in coats and hats and scarves, but Jacob, the college junior with a mind of his own, only wore jeans, a T-shirt, and a sweatshirt with the logo for an entity named Sparco on it, an aftermarket Japanese gearhead company he seems to worship. In the photo you can see he's cold, his hands jammed into his pockets, shoulders up as high as he can get them.

We walked through security, a sort of steel lobby with a guard behind a thick glass window who looked at each of our passports, looked at us, then nodded us through, we four emerging on the other side to a gang of shouting cabbies, all eager to drive us anywhere we wanted.

We chose an older man who looked a great deal like Yasser Arafat, with his red and white keffiyeh and grizzled beard. He'd seemed quieter than the rest, a little more reserved—and therefore, to be honest, less threatening. We were alone and where we shouldn't be, and toting our son and my mother too.

But once we were packed into the cab, the man seemed revived, boisterous, a little too loud. At first he headed up Hebron Road, same as the first time we'd been here, all the while talking about the number of Americans he drove every day, the sites he'd take us to, his cousin with the shop right next to the Church of the Nativity.

And though we'd told him we wanted only to go to the church, he decided there were other places we needed to see, what he called the Christian Sites tour, and then he turned left off Hebron onto a road we hadn't been on before, then turned down another, and headed away from town, into the desert. I glanced to the backseat—I was in the front seat—to see my son and mother taking in the streets, the desert, this adventure. But Melanie's eyes were locked on mine, telling me what I already knew: We'd lost control of what was going on.

Yet a piece of me kept feeling safe, kept feeling we would be all right. An American family wasn't going to disappear in Bethlehem. But another, larger part let my heartbeat gain on me, until when we pulled into the parking lot of the Greek Orthodox Church of the Shepherds' Fields I could feel my palms sweating. Once we were out of the taxi, the driver leading us on into the church, Melanie and I had a close conversation about the whole thing, and decided we'd have to take back this excursion. I'd tell him—I'd insist—we only wanted to go see the Church of the Nativity, and then head back to the wall. That was all. End of trip.

We walked through the limestone Church of the Shepherds' Fields, built on one of the traditional sites where the angels appeared to the shepherds to herald Christ's birth. Though constructed only in 1989, the interior was extraordinary for its Byzantine-like figures on the walls, the ceilings, everywhere. Skulls of monks killed by the Persians in 614 as part of the destruction of the original monastery were on display in glass cases, three separate altars dedicated each to the Holy Mother, to Saint Panteleimon (whose neck, when the executioner tried to behead him, bent the sword), and to the angels Gabriel and Michael and the heavenly host that appeared to the shepherds in the night above Bethlehem.

Outside were olive trees, ancient with trunks as big around as a VW, signs posted attesting to their having been here since before the birth of Christ. A covered pavilion protected mosaic floors and foundations left of the earliest church from the fourth century, and the Byzantine chapel destroyed in the fifth century, and the monastery destroyed in the seventh.

But an edged-up adrenalin jagged through me the whole time, Melanie and I exchanging looks while the driver pointed to this stained glass, that carved and time-worn capital, this olive tree. And when, finally, we climbed back in the cab, I told him as flatly as I could, as clearly as I could, we'd had enough touring. We wanted, just like we'd told him already, only to go to the Church of the Nativity.

He seemed a little let down, looked at me from behind the wheel with his eyebrows up. He shrugged, put the car in gear, and we headed off, away from the desert spread out behind the church, and up into the winding streets of Bethlehem.

We took one side street, and another one, narrower, and yet another, even narrower, until I had no idea where we were in relation to the church itself. Though I'd been there only once, I knew from the drive in with our friend that we stayed on Hebron and had headed up and up, more buildings closing in around us, then took only one street off Hebron and followed it until we came out onto Manger Square, the broad plaza lined with shops, at one end the church itself with its distinctive arched belltower, beneath it the nondescript walls of the church some thirty or forty feet high.

But this wasn't the route at all.

Finally, after turn and turn and turn, the street we were on no more than an alley, the driver nudged the car up beside a stone building. He put the cab in park, then turned to me, smiled. "One last place we go before church," he said. "My cousin have shop. We go here. Then church." He looked out the windshield, nodded quick at the building.

Here was a green metal awning perched above the doorway in, the green door opened out and on it two long black dresses, the cuffs and necklines and bodices embroidered in bright colors.

I leaned farther forward, looked out the windshield at the sign above the awning: OLD CAVE SOUVENIR.

"Hey!" I nearly shouted. "We know this place!" and I felt a kind of steadying wash through me, let out a breath I hadn't known I was holding in. There were good people in there: the family who'd known our friend the Baptist missionary all these years.

The driver looked at me, no expression to him at all. He blinked, said quietly, "Is my cousin," then popped open his door.

I glanced back at Melanie who seemed almost ready—but not quite—to smile. Jacob opened his door, and he and my mother and my wife all climbed out, followed our driver in. "We need to talk to them," Melanie whispered to me as we headed through those front doors and inside.

The family—the mother, her two sons, only one grandchild this time—were all there, same as before, and the driver started in on them in Arabic, then English, introducing us to them as his cousins, and what a marvelous shop this was, how historic, the oldest one in Bethlehem.

But the older son, then the mother, then the other son and the granddaughter all recognized us before he was finished, and brushed past the driver to welcome us: handshakes between the brothers and Jacob and I, short bows to and from the women. The granddaughter disappeared to go make coffee, the mother brought us to the same chairs we'd sat in before, and seemed genuinely interested in my mother and Jacob, smiled and nodded and asked questions of how they were. The younger son stepped back out through the doors and to the street, headed perhaps for the workshop itself in the cave beneath the building.

And inside this commotion of what felt a surprise visit, I saw the older son look to the driver and nod to follow him, all very careful, all very inconspicuous. But I was watching. Because it seemed, in this refreshing grace the family offered, the relief this place gave, that something was going on.

The two moved off to the corner of the room crowded with all its olive wood nativities and ornaments and decorations, and the older son seemed nearly to pin the driver to the wall. He spoke quickly and quietly to him, the driver silent, looking up at him, his mouth a thin line. He said nothing.

A moment later and they were done. The son turned back to us, smiling. He ran a hand back through his hair, asked about our friend the missionary and how he was doing, while now the granddaughter brought in coffee on what looked the same tray as before, the same tiny handleless cups filled with that sweet and bitter coffee.

If the driver had seemed a little let down back in the cab when we'd told him to take us straight to the Church of the Nativity, he was completely deflated now. Empty. He didn't move out of the corner, said nothing, only stood with his arms crossed, his eyes down.

My mother and Jacob began looking through things, careful with their cups, and touched at palm tree and camel ornaments, marveled at carved and painted and elaborate nativities, while Melanie and I went to the son, stood perhaps a little too close to him.

He was smiling, but it seemed a nervous smile, a preoccupied one, maybe, and I went ahead and said quietly, "This driver is taking us places we don't want to go. We're happy to be here—very happy—" I smiled hard at him, but truly, to make him know we were in fact very glad to be here. "But he's taking us places we don't want to go."

"Bret's mom and our son are with us," Melanie said quietly then, and the son looked at her, the smile seeming now to fade. "We just want to go to the church and then go home," she said.

He nodded then, pursed his lips and glanced over his shoulder, back to where the driver still stood, still with eyes down, arms crossed. Then he turned back to us. "Okay," he said. "I will take you there."

We couldn't believe this good news, this generosity. "Really?" we pressed. "Really?" and he smiled openly then, nodded again and again.

"But we need to go now," he said, and started for the doorway. "Please," he said, "this way," and nodded again, this time to my mother and to Jacob, who both finished off their coffees, set their cups on the tray at the counter. They thanked the mother, and the granddaughter, and moved toward the door.

The son looked back at the driver, still in place, said quick words to him in Arabic, and finally the man nodded, whatever they spoke about decided. He didn't move.

"Can we come back to buy some things?" my mother said as we moved out onto the narrow street, the high stone walls around us making the alley seem even narrower than before. Jacob, hands in his pockets for the cold, moved out to the center of the alley, turned and looked at us, as did my mother, wondering, I could see, what was the rush.

"Sure," I said, and looked at the son, who smiled, nodded, said, "Yes of course!" He was already past Jacob now, headed to the limestone wall across from the store, where, I only now saw, was a green door, tall, old, weathered. It stood at the top of three or four limestone steps, and was wider than a simple doorway, more imposing in its way: an entryway into something else. The son quickly took the steps up, pulled from his pocket a set of keys, then put his hand to the old latch, unlocked and opened the door and waved us in.

At that moment, out there on the street, I thought I could hear from somewhere someone on a loudspeaker. Somewhere away from here, but a voice. This was almost Christmas, and maybe there was some sort of celebration out on Manger Square, some call to tourists to visit the shops out there on the plaza.

Inside the doorway was a courtyard thirty or forty feet across, all paved with stone, high walls all around, with what looked like a turret of sorts directly across from us. To the right were more stone steps up, these in a half-circle against the wall there, at its top black double doors, tall too. Another entryway.

"We go in this way," the son said, and led us across the courtyard to those steps and up to the door. He opened it, waved us in again, but this time his moves slower, careful, his cupped hand calling us in a bit more tentatively. He stood just inside, the room he was in dark, and he glanced to his right, nodded at someone, it seemed, then looked out to us again, smiling. All of it so quiet I could hear that loudspeaker—a bullhorn?—and that speaker even clearer.

My mother, then Jacob and Melanie headed up, disappeared inside, and then I stepped in, the son holding the door for me.

We were in a narrow and nearly dark room, the ceiling and walls all wood, all black, what felt almost a cloak room save for its height, and then the son led us through another door into a larger room, and suddenly, strangely, beautifully, we were, as though by a gift of grace, inside the Church of the Nativity.

This was the transept—that place that seemed from out in the courtyard a turret—before us the high altar itself, with its gold and candles and carved wood and intricacies beyond intricacies: Rows of silver and gold icons, hanging glass and gold lamps, marble floors inlaid in green and red and white. Incense burning.

I took in a breath, smelled the age and majesty and humility of this place, all inside the scent of this incense. We were safe.

I turned to my mother, and to Jacob. My mother's mouth was open, and she blinked, took in a quiet gasp—joy, I could see—then whispered, "Are we here?"

"Yes," Melanie whispered from beside her, and Jacob, hands out of his pockets now and at his sides, whispered, "Wow."

And I could see behind them, back near the door we had come in, the son. He was speaking to a priest standing in the corner, someone we'd passed right by, taken in as we were with being here, right here. The priest wore a black robe and had a heavy beard, on his head a black pillbox sort of hat. His hands were together in front of him, his mouth in a grimace, eyes on the son.

Then the priest closed his eyes a moment, opened them, and nodded slowly. He smiled, held out a hand to the son, and they shook, the son nodding again and again and smiling himself.

We'd come in the back door to the Church of the Nativity. Let in by the son, with the ex post facto permission of the priest at the door.

We moved out into the sanctuary then, with its twin rows of ancient pillars varnished with centuries of incense and candle smoke, the ceiling sooted with centuries of that smoke too. Trap doors lay open along the floor to reveal mosaic sub-floors, crisp geometric patterns and birds and fish and grapes; on the walls above the pillars we could make out scenes from Christ's life in colored and gold-leafed mosaics, sooted too.

My mother, in her coat and scarf tied at her chin, purse crooked in her arm, walked through it all, quiet. Jacob in his Sparco sweatshirt walked on his own, stopping to touch one of the pillars where the impression of a cross the size of his hand had been dug in, as though a crucifix had been embedded there and torn away a long time ago.

Then we four went to the right of the altar, and took the steep stone stairs down a narrow passageway and to the Grotto below the altar, that place on planet Earth, bedecked with velvet and gold and candles, where it is believed Christ was born. We'd lingered there a while among ten or twenty people packed into a cave not much bigger than a good-sized kitchen; I took a great many photos of my mother, and my son, my wife, and of the polished marble hearth-like shrine with its starburst silver inlay, at its center a small hole into which one puts a hand to feel the ground there: the spot where Jesus first appeared. Then we left, went up a second set of stone steps that came out on the left side of the altar, where stood the son, waiting for us.

"I want to go through the front door to show my mom," I said. "The Door of Humility."

He glanced down the sanctuary toward the four-foot door at the far end of the church, then looked back at us. "If this is what you want," he said. He had his hands in his back pockets, and gave a quick shrug. Maybe too quick.

He seemed nervous.

We walked down the sanctuary, through its calm and beauty and age. We took in one last time these pillars, the mosaic sub-floors, the gold-leaf mosaics, and then we were at the low doorway, built that way, our friend had told us our first time here, because raiders made a practice of charging into the original church on horseback, destroying anything they found. A four foot tall door meant you had to bend over, make yourself vulnerable—humble—as you entered into the place where the Prince of Peace was born.

The son went out first, then my mother, Jacob, Melanie, and then me, all of us crouched down for it, all of us humbled for it, and finally out onto Manger Square.

Here was that voice, that loudspeaker, shouted words jumbled, loud.

Out in the plaza, maybe a hundred yards away, swarmed a thick knot of people, shouting. A couple hundred people, and now the one yelling into the loudspeaker—invisible inside the crowd—began a chant, the crowd shouting back a response. And in among them, waving sharp swaths through the air, were green flags with Arabic printed in white, the jumble of marks at its center the Shahada, the Muslim profession of faith: There is no god but Allah, and Muhammad is the messenger of Allah.

These were rally flags for Hamas. The more militant party of the Palestinian Authority, more so than Fatah, with whom it was in conflict right then for control of Gaza and the West Bank. Hamas: the group responsible for the most suicide bombings in the latest intifada.

The son of the prime minister of the Palestinian Authority, a Hamas party member, had been shot yesterday down at the border with Egypt, his bodyguard killed. Hamas assigned Fatah the blame.

I read the news. But that day I was just taking my family to Bethlehem. All that violence was down at the Gaza border with Egypt.

The speaker shouted again, the crowd shouted back. Those flags waved, it seemed, even more sharply back and forth.

I looked to the son, all of us there in front of the Door of Humility. His eyes were on the crowd, and he ran a hand back through his hair again, put his hands in his back pockets again. His mouth was pursed, his eyebrows furrowed.

"Umm," I said.

"We go back the way we came," he said, still with his eyes on the crowd just over there, right over there. "We will be safe."

This was when things fell together in me: the son confronting the driver back in the corner of the shop, those hard words that must have been *Why did you bring them here? Don't you know what is happening today?* Then in through the back door, all with his nervous smile, his quick shrug, his hand back through his hair.

The son, I understood then, was doing his best to guard us here in the West Bank. On this side of the wall.

Morning traffic grows thick the deeper into Ramallah we go, until we're stopped altogether, around us trucks and cars and motorcycles. Out my window I can see how the city is built on a hill, apartment buildings terraced down its side. Out Moshe's window is a grocery store, *Supermarket Baghdad* in bright green and red neon letters above the front doors. Above us a banner stretches across the street advertising a bank—I only know this from the website in small print at the bottom—with pictures of a group of young people smiling and cheering, fists in the air in triumph. One of them holds a drum. In front of us is a blue Cadbury Dairy Milk delivery van, on its rear doors painted a smooth wave of cream, beneath it a square of white chocolate.

"Houston, approach," Moshe says into the mic, and "Roger" comes back immediately. Akeem says from the back seat, "Almost there."

Traffic budges a bit, and then at the next left we turn onto a smaller street, beside us those apartment buildings quickly giving way to lower buildings. More shops, and now what seems a residence with laundry hanging out to dry on the second floor patio. We turn left again, and the street narrows to an alley only wide enough to walk. Moshe pulls to a stop on the right beside a white limestone residence, an awning out front.

Before us, where the street becomes a walkway, the stones that make up the low walls and the buildings are old. Very old. As in limestone worn to brown, the edges worn away. Old.

"Here we go," Akeem says, pops open his door and climbs out. Maryam scoots across and out his door, and I am left to push open mine then too, push with both hands this bulletproof door it had taken two hands to pull open.

I'd made a joke when I'd done that, an hour ago out front of the consulate. A joke that seems, now, even smaller than when I'd said it.

Before I close it, I look back in at Moshe. He's still behind the wheel, his door closed.

"You coming in?" I say, and he gives a small smile, shakes his head. I can't see his eyes—haven't seen them yet—for those aviator sunglasses he wears, but I see now he doesn't look like Zoolander at all with that spiky hair, those sunglasses.

He's a man doing his job.

"I be out here," he says. "I wait."

We cross the street to the old old walls there, and enter through a doorway with what appears to be a Knights Templar cross carved into the lintel. Inside is a smart, stylish, modern office, a large desk cluttered with papers. Behind it and standing from her chair now to greet us is the publisher, a woman in a black jersey and black pants, brown hair. With her is a young woman in a white blouse and skirt with a black string tie, her assistant, and introductions are made all around, pleasantries exchanged, a hug given between Maryam and the publisher who, it is revealed, have known each other for some time.

On the walls are framed covers for children's books they've published, and original illustrations, all elegant and simple. The floor is paved with traditional tiles, geometric patterns in red and white, black and pale blue, framing them all a rim of tiles with green grape leaves, red vines.

We all move from the desk then, and take seats in padded office chairs to the left that casually encircle a low glass table in the middle, upon the table a white plate of the most exquisite fruit I have ever seen.

I am not being hyperbolic. I mean this.

This city has been a surprise—its citiness, its modern presence on an ancient hill. As much a surprise as a crusader cross carved above a doorway, and the fact there is an extraction team somewhere, watching this place and us in it, and the surprise of a man named Moshe who sits outside and waits for us. All surprises for reasons I cannot say other than that Ramallah has always existed as a place of trepidation, however much I have buried that feeling, hidden it away with my small joke at riding shotgun, my out-loud laugh at a coffee shop bold enough to make no bones about ripping off Starbucks.

But this plate of fruit seems a kind of miracle, for no other reason than that it is beautiful, and simple, and true.

The fruit: A handful of fresh red cherries, their stems thin grace notes of green; five apples, each one a rich eddy of light green and deep red; eight or ten baby cucumbers, shiny and perfect and cucumber green.

We talk about how children here are underserved when it comes to books about their own lives, their identities, their homeland, their government; about the reading centers and their popularity not just in Ramallah but in other cities in Gaza and the West Bank; about nurturing new writers; about new books coming out soon.

A woman comes into the room at one point with a tray of coffee and tea both, the coffee in porcelain cups, the tea in glass teacups, handles included with both. I choose a coffee, and sip at it, black and bittersweet.

I am handed books, look through them, entirely impressed. Printed in English and Arabic both, they tell stories of girls and boys and hills and olives and animals and the ocean and desert. They are beautiful, colorful, excellently produced. Artistic and accessible, meaningful and playful. Good.

Still we talk, though mostly I listen. But I am listening to a good story of good news. A story of hope, and creation, and why the imagination matters. Why books and why reading matter, and I can see throughout this story the care they give this community, the craft with which they make their art, the love they have for this all.

I have brought books of my own as gifts, though they seem paltry and inappropriate—I am not being falsely modest, here in the light of this program, these people—and I sign them to her and to her assistant, and now in just these few moments of listening more than an hour has already passed, all of us up now and taking pictures to record this event.

Reading, we understand between us, matters. Words placed one after another matter. Books allow the imagination—and so hope, and peace, and justice—to envision what can be.

But before I leave I tell her how beautiful the plate of fruit is.

The publisher immediately tells me I am welcome to any of it, and I tell her no, thank you, but can I take a picture of them?

She gives a small laugh at this, as does her assistant, and Akeem and Maryam both do too. A polite acknowledgment of the strangeness—maybe silliness—of this request by the visiting American writer, and I take a photo of them on my iPhone.

It seems, in some small way, a metaphor of sorts, a symbol, though of what at that moment I cannot say. But these cherries, these apples and cucumbers, their colors at this particular moment, their arrangement on a white plate that is no arrangement other than that of fresh fruit upon it, is something to behold.

Perhaps peace. Maybe promise. Possibly hope.

Then we are away, because we have other places to go. Maryam and the publisher give each other another hug, and Akeem leads us from this elegant office and the publisher and her assistant outside to these ancient limestone walls, while just across the street a silver Suburban sits waiting.

Moshe, behind the wheel and with the window open, smiles at us, nods.

I pause then, look up at the buildings around us, the low white limestone residences two and three stories tall, just beyond them and to my right the high-rise we'd turned past onto the street that led to this one.

Where, I wonder, would an extraction team be right now? And can they see me down here, wondering about them?

Back inside Old Cave Souvenir, my mother looked for things to buy. She still had her scarf on, knotted at the chin, and her coat. Jacob, hands back in his pockets, leaned in to different nativities now and again, took in the details.

The driver, with his grizzled beard and red and white keffiyeh, still leaned against the back wall, same as before. In front of him the son spoke quietly to him, less exuberantly now, less stressed, it seemed.

He turned from the driver then, looked at us from across the store. He smiled, gave a serious nod. "Everything is okay," he said.

Melanie and I nodded at him in the same moment, and I turned to my mother and Jacob, said, "All right, time to head on back." In the next few minutes my mother selected a half-dozen olive wood ornaments to buy, and Melanie picked some out too, though we'd already been here before, already bought that nativity. But she needed to buy something, I knew, as a means to say thank you.

The mother, behind the counter, placed our goods into bags, smiling and wishing us all well, wishing us a Merry Christmas, wishing us a safe journey home, and the driver finally pushed himself from the wall and walked out the door ahead of us.

He still hadn't said a word.

The son followed us out, and my family climbed into the backseat of the cab. But before I got in, I looked at the son, said, "Thank you. Thank you. Thank you. Shukran. Shukran. Shukran."

He laughed then, nodded. "Afwan!" he said. "You will be safe. He is taking you back now. Direct."

"Thank you, " I said one more time, then, "God bless you."

He waved, headed back in to the store.

The driver backed out of the alley and onto the wider street he'd come in on, then drove down the maze of streets back toward the wall, down from the hilltop where the church stood. Between buildings now and again I could see the desert down there, stretching to the east. Down where the angels appeared to the shepherds. Down where we'd already been.

The driver said nothing all the way back to the wall, only dropped us off at the security checkpoint, where I paid him the agreed upon fee. "Thank you," I said to him, and he nodded, our eyes never meeting.

Then we turned to that portal, and walked back through, past guards and glass and steel, our passports out. Same as when we'd arrived, we seasoned travelers.

That night we watched the news, just in case there was something about what we saw. Nothing about Bethlehem, but in Ramallah, Hamas staged a march through downtown, where they were met by Palestinian riot police with rifles and clubs. Twelve people had been shot. We watched the footage: attacks in the streets at midday, guns fired in the air, clubs swinging, people tackled and beaten.

Moshe heads back out to the main road with its billboards and sidewalks and landscaped median, words and words and words passed between us of, indeed, the good work the institute is doing for its people.

But we're headed now in a different direction, not the way we came. We see a little more of this city—more high-rises, more buildings tiered down the hillside—and then we come to another roundabout, where three-fourths of the way through we are slingshotted out into desert again. It's a small road, an unobtrusive one. A back road.

Along the shoulder now are people working vegetable and fruit stands, the stalls with make-shift umbrellas, tarps, anything to get out of the sun, beneath them stacks of plastic crates filled with tomatoes, corn, onions. A pickup truck is backed up to the roadside, in its bed a pyramid of perfect round watermelons, a small triangle of rind cut out of most of them to show how red and ripe they are. Cars are pulled over, people looking, touching, buying.

Desert all around.

Akeem says, "Lunch!" and I see up ahead on the right a low flat build-ing, a couple cars parked in the dirt lot out front, and Moshe puts on the blinker, slows down as we approach. "This is the best *sfiha* in the world," Akeem says.

"The best what?" I say, and turn, look at him.

He's sitting up straight in his seat and leaned forward, smiling, a hand to the top of my own seat: a kid pulling up to McDonald's. "Sfee-*ha*," is what I hear when he says it again, and he glances at me, sees by the empty look on my face I still don't get it.

"It's like pizza," he says. "But better. You can get some other toppings. But this guy's *sfiha* is delicious. It's like a flatbread with ground lamb and spices and pine nuts."

He's nodding as he talks, excited. Then he says this, spoken by a South Carolina-born former Army Ranger:

"My mom used to make it. This is like being back home."

And then Bethlehem-born Maryam says, "My mother makes it too," and nods, smiling.

I can see the bakery up on the right, a storefront in a one-story limestone building, glass windows and a door. Moshe pulls up, puts the

Suburban in park, and Akeem says to him something, Moshe with a one-word answer: "*Sfiha.*"

Akeem is taking his order, I see. Because Moshe can't leave the vehicle, I finally see too.

He's Security.

We climb out, and Akeem and Maryam head in.

But I stop for a moment, look across the hood of the Suburban to the desert over there, and I put up a hand to block the midday sun.

The desert slopes gently down from the street to what looks like a cement plant, or perhaps a quarry, a white pit in a kind of shallow valley maybe five hundred yards off. Between here and there are structures, scaffolds, heaps of white. A hill rises on the other side, and just past it, over the horizon, are the tops of apartment high-rises, a long low line of them.

But there, at the bottom of the valley, nearly camouflaged in the brown-beige of the desert, runs the brown-beige surprise of the Separation Barrier. The wall.

It's a perfect line across the whole of my line of sight, a slow easy arc one side to the other, dipping slightly down to follow the contours of this valley at the center. A brown-beige ribbon all the way across. Hard to see for the light, and the structures, the quarry, those apartments above the hill across this valley.

Not what I was expecting to see. Not what I was looking for. I just wanted to take in the desert, the land, this place. To remember it.

And so, as with that plate of fruit, I get out my iPhone, take a picture. A panorama, to try and get in the whole of all I can see here.

We are very far from everything, it seems. Here's the desert. Here's a wall.

But it's only eight miles from here to Jerusalem. Eight miles in a straight line. Not far at all.

I turn from the view, glance at Moshe behind the wheel, always behind the wheel, and smile. He gives me the thumbs up, and I nod, head inside to what feels like a take-out pizza place, the room warm, humid, close.

Two men work behind the counter, pressing dough into rounds eight or ten inches across. The older, in a white dress shirt, two pens in his front pocket, is already talking to Akeem, and I can tell they know each other by the ease of their words, the nods, smiles. This place has to be a regular stop for him every time he brings someone in to Ramallah.

The man stops and wipes his hands on his white apron, and gives a kind of short bow to Maryam—I hear her name in amongst Akeem's deft tangle of words—and then up pops my name too, and the man puts out his hand, and we shake. He points now to the younger man—so obviously his son it doesn't bear remark—who has on a blue polo and who glances up from his work at Akeem, nods and says a quick something, then nods to Maryam and to me.

He turns then to the oven behind him. The front is only a fake stone façade, it's easy to tell, maybe eight feet tall, ten feet wide, perfect flat stones in a repeated pattern that runs across the top and down either side. Otherwise, the oven is open from the floor up to where that façade begins across the top, no chest high oven mouth to slide in these pizza-like things. Instead a kind of metal frame four feet tall sits in there, on top of it a large square baking sheet, on it eight or nine of these pizzas—these *sfihas*?

They look like personal pizzas, but different. There's no red sauce, no pepperonis or mushrooms or onions, but only a thick slathering of brown topping, a solid layer of it, the only dough visible the half-inch crust.

Just past the tray, deep inside this strange oven contraption, is the heat itself, what looks like charcoal banked up, and hot. I can feel it shimmering out at us, and then the son touches the baking sheet in there with his fingers, quick pushes in at one side, pulls out the other, spinning the tray until the *sfihas* that were next to the heat are now on this side.

He does this in an instant, no hot pads or a towel or tongs or anything. Just his fingers, the whole tray of sfihas turned. He hasn't even stopped paying attention to the talk going on between Akeem and his father and Maryam, his eyes on them.

Akeem and the father talk, the son and Maryam talk, then Akeem says something else, and all four of them—Akeem, Maryam, the father, the son—turn and look at me, the sudden center of whatever words have passed between them.

Maybe he's told them I'm the writer here from America, I'm thinking. Maybe he's told them of the mission we're on, how we've met with the publisher at the institute in downtown Ramallah to talk about books.

They are all quiet a second, all looking at me, and I nod, smile at the father and son, nod again.

"What do you want to order?" Akeem says.

"Oh!" I say. "Okay," I say, and smile harder, embarrassed at what I figure I have missed, watching the son tend to the oven, these pizzas.

"What you're having," I say, and nod. "Safeeya?"

They all laugh then. Even Maryam.

But here's the thing: here's the thing: It isn't a mocking laugh, or one meant to ridicule. It isn't sharp or loud, isn't at my expense. It is only a laugh at the word I said, the whatever-way I garbled the simple two-syllable name of what looks like a very good thing to eat.

"*Sfiha*," the father says, on his face an easy smile, and the son echoes him, says, quieter, "*Sfiha*."

"We'll work on your pronunciation," Akeem says, then, "You're going to love this," and Maryam says, "Yes," all smiles everywhere, and the father and son set to work placing balls of dough onto another of those baking trays.

Here's the thing: I'm safe.

Not for the fact of a Suburban waiting outside, or an advance team somewhere ahead of us and out of sight, or an extraction team hidden somewhere too.

And not for the fact of a wall I will be heading to soon, where on the other side I won't have Moshe and bulletproof doors.

But because of words, and what they can do when aligned with hope, and vision, and love, and exchanged with good will between us. Even if, sometimes, they're mispronounced.

The father and son are almost finished putting our *sfihas* together: they're ladling on that lamb meat with its spices, its pine nuts, spreading round the dough the rich brown paste, finishing up with these mementoes of home before going into that oven.

This is going to be good. I can tell.

Olives in Jerusalem

DRIVERS HERE BELIEVE in the car horn. They've deemed it a primary feature, as much a part of the endeavor as the gas pedal. Many are the times—and I mean many—when we have been sitting in Jerusalem traffic, before us a line of stopped cars snaked up the street as far as anyone can see, and someone behind us lays in on the horn.

And always, in a kind of loudmouth retort to that frustrated call, someone else lays in, and another, and bright blistering noise erupts all around us. Every time.

And still we sit in traffic.

Stoplights here are different too: The green light begins to flash when it's about to turn yellow, then the yellow light beneath it comes on for a brief moment, then comes the red; when the red light is about to change, the yellow light goes on right above it so that for some three seconds the red and yellow show at the same time. Then those lights shut off and the green comes back on.

What drivers have decided here, though, is that the red and yellow light showing just before the green comes on means *Go*, and they go. Period. How this relates to the horn as a tool for driving is that precisely when the yellow light comes on above the red, long before the electrical circuit that connects the green light even goes off—I mean this—as soon as the yellow goes on beneath the red, the driver behind you honks. And he honks *even if you are already moving forward in anticipation of that green light showing up some time soon.*

We've driven in a lot of places. Paris, Florence, Rome. Dublin and Izmir, Monaco and Glasgow, Frankfurt and Naples. Cancun and Quebec. Anchorage and the Hana Highway. Manhattan and Los Angeles (where I learned to drive on the freeways), Seattle and Chicago and Houston and Miami and the worst city in the world to drive, Boston.

And nowhere—nowhere—do they honk the horn like they do in Jerusalem.

Here they honk if you leave a few feet between you and the car ahead of you at a light, and if you're not going fast enough through that light, and if you slow down when that yellow below the green comes on. They honk at you if you put your blinker on while sitting at a curb and just beginning to *think* of pulling into traffic, and when you use your blinker to begin a lane change, and when you use your blinker to turn a corner.

The blinker, by the way, is never used. Maybe because of its location in the car, sort of buried behind the steering wheel, hidden on the column, and so of what importance could that thing be? Not like this horn, front and center in the cockpit of my car, an important tool I must have to use because it's so central to everything, and handy!

Then there's the driving itself, the overriding ethos not *Safety first!* but *Me first!* Drivers cut in line and cut in line and cut in line, no matter if you're on the freeway or in a grocery store parking lot. When we lived there, a stretch of road on the block behind our apartment on Emek Refaim was torn up for nearly a month, a half mile stretch integral to our driving life, as it was the route we had to take to get to our parking space behind the apartment building. Each time we came home from anywhere we had to drive a big rectangular loop around the neighborhood, crossing the railroad tracks behind our building, though when we parked we were only about a hundred yards from the apartment.

For days and days they repaved that street, one of those gargantuan asphalt paving machines riding down the middle of the road and laying asphalt, smoke and steam and workers with shovels everywhere. This on a street only wide enough on a normal day to allow two lanes of traffic to squeeze through.

But there was never anyone guiding traffic, we drivers left to figure out how to go around it.

Which meant every driver for himself, everyone cutting in around the oily commotion, everyone honking horns to let *me!* through, all fighting their way back and forth around the whole thing. Just mass chaos, drivers cutting each other off time and again and time and again.

Balagan is the Hebrew word for it, a Russian-rooted loanword used all the time to describe any given situation in which chaos reigns, from everyday traffic to the line at Café Hillel for a coffee to the standard-issue walkouts and shouting matches at the Knesset. The word gets used all the time, most often accompanied by a shrug, a tilt of the head, hands out to the side: *Oh well. What can you do.*

It's a word we used a lot.

One morning in particular came a series of events that made me believe I was in some kind of live driver's ed film. I was a couple blocks off Emek Refaim on a residential street there in German Colony, hoping to find a shortcut to avoid the eternal traffic on the main drag. Suddenly, in the oncoming traffic, the car behind the car coming toward me pulled out into my lane and passed him, this only about fifty feet ahead of me. Then, in the next moment, a car parked at the curb to my right pulled directly out in front of me, and in the next—this is literal, this is true—another car there at the curb popped open his door so that I had to swerve to the left and into more oncoming traffic then back into my lane. In the next moment a woman pushing a baby in a stroller—there are a million women pushing strollers here, the nation of Israel truly fruitful and multiplying—strode out from between two parked cars to my left and into the street and oncoming traffic, me included.

All of this in about ten seconds.

Balagan.

I told this all to Donald and Linda over dinner at their house one night not long after. I complained. I railed. I shook my head at how crazy the drivers were, the traffic, the reliance upon and utter ineffectiveness of these badgering horns. I railed too about the way people cut into lines no matter the venue, whether the post office or for my coffee or even standing with a grocery cart and obviously next in line for the cashier. It didn't matter where. People cut in line, and I went on a tear about Sabras and how that whole prickly on the outside but sweet on the inside stuff was probably a bunch of hooey. Let somebody merge in now again. Prove that sweet inside. Lay off the horn. Use your blinker.

Wise, calm, chuckling Donald—he always seemed to be quietly chuckling whenever I tried to say something about life in Israel—only shook his head, eased back in his chair there at the table. "You don't get it," he said. "Cutting in line is a virtue. Nobody wants to be a *freier.*"

"A what?" I'd asked, and thought at once of two things: chicken bought at the grocery store, whole fryers; and monks with their tonsures, Friar Tuck and all that.

He'd gone on then in his wise and calm and chuckling way to educate us on the concept of the *freier,* the sucker, the loser, and why not being one was a raison d'être of Israeli life. Nobody wanted to be taken advantage of—look at the history of the Jews for a clear reason why—and so to take advantage of another in the everyday of life was seen as a worthy and laudatory and virtuous goal. To be taken advantage of, he told us, was seen as a kind of sin. Being a *freier* was being a loser. So one *had* to cut in. One *had* to be virtuous.

He chuckled. And he told me too the Sabra thing was true. Just watch for it.

With that news—troubling news for we soft Americans who'd always thought a line was a fixed and uninterrupted vector—many many things came into focus. Not that we were promptly going to embrace this antonymic definition of virtuous behavior. No. But something gave way a little bit, and now the gnarled mobs for coffee, and the free-for-all at the post office, and the way the hostess at a restaurant simply ignored you when somebody pushed in front of you and started right in in Hebrew, all made a kind of sense.

Balagan, we saw now, was engendered by not wanting to be a *freier*; not wanting to be a *freier* engendered acting in a way that brought about the *balagan* of it all. A nice, tidy, self-contained system of perpetual chaotic virtue.

But what else could happen than that this new understanding brought about our slowly giving in?

We started using the horn. Small taps, a little touch here and there. No big barks but the tiniest nips now and again. At Café Hillel I shouldered off—gently—people pushing in at the edges to make their coffee order. At the post office I raised my voice to keep the attention of the worker behind the counter.

Then my virtue deepened even further: I stopped letting anyone merge into my lane. I stopped using the blinker. I cut in, and cut in, and cut in, the roadway one long cage-match on my quest for upright living.

And I began to feel myself acclimate to this brand of virtue. To become a Jerusalem driver, someone who wouldn't be taken advantage of. I started to feel as though I were on my way to being a non-*freier*, the horn a sort of language everyone here spoke, me beginning to utter it too. First in a whisper, but then full-voiced and hearty.

No *freier* was I going to be.

But then.

One autumn evening we were yet again mired in that dumb circuit we had to drive to get to our parking area. Melanie had come with me down to Bar-Ilan for the day, hung out on campus to take photos while I taught. The drive up from Tel Aviv took about an hour until as always, here in the last approach to home, things turned bad, the neighborhood always heavy with traffic. We just wanted to get home, go get some falafel and shawarma laffa at Doron, then sit and watch TV, the both of us tired at the end of this day.

Then traffic stopped fully. This was the next to last leg of the circle, where the road was narrowest, no room for cars to park on either side of the street, only a sidewalk and cinderblock wall on the passenger side, the sidewalk dotted every twenty yards or so with an olive tree for landscaping.

I honked the horn. I wanted badly to pass the guy ahead of me, to get at least one car length ahead of myself. Traffic was solid both ways, but that didn't matter. I wanted to bark, and so I barked. Then again.

Finally the car in front of me moved a bit, and stopped, moved a few feet again, and stopped, we all literally inching along.

And it occurred to me no one had joined in my honk. No shouted response to my call. No bark back. Nothing.

It was dusk, the sky above us the deepest blue, and I turned on our headlights, and just as I did I could see ahead of me a strange and bewildering traffic configuration, like nothing I'd seen in Jerusalem before: there seemed to be something in the road ahead that made each car in my lane pull into the left lane, pass by it, then swing back into this right lane. And traffic in the oncoming lane let them, politely alternating car by car by car.

People were behaving. People were taking turns. No one honked.

Maybe there was a crash up there, I thought. Maybe someone hurt, everyone quiet for it. But no. There were no police cars with their bright blue strobing lights, no EMS. Only cars alternating around something up there.

Then it was my turn, the car ahead of me allowed to pull to the left and around what was in the street by the next oncoming car, and I saw the holdup at the center of everything.

Here on the right was a Bedouin family, working at harvesting olives from a tree on the sidewalk. They'd laid out old sheets and ragged quilts beneath the tree, the sidewalk and a few feet out into the street covered by them.

Olives, I could see in the headlights, lay sprinkled across them all.

A woman in a long black dress, a black scarf wound around her head, stood a foot or so off the curb and in the street, peering up into the branches. In her hands was a long stick up in there, the woman shaking it. Two kids sat on plastic crates against the cinderblock wall on the other side of the sidewalk. Against the trunk leaned a ladder, on its uppermost step the black-sandaled feet and black pantlegs of a man, up there and working.

We'd seen this before, not long ago on one of our afternoon walks to Bloomfield Garden, with its view of the Old City, and its rosemary, its limestone pathways. And its olive trees.

It was the sheet and blankets I'd seen first, laid out beneath one of the trees, a puzzling thing: a neat square of old material laid out precisely around an olive tree. A woman in her *madraga*, that long black dress the Bedouin women wore, and wearing the head wrap, an *usaba*, worked a stick up in the branches, same as here. Four kids sat on crates just as these two did here on the street, dressed in worn out sweaters and jeans. But I could see the father at the top of the ladder in that tree, his black sandals and dusty black pants, his gray suit coat, white shirt underneath, and the white keffiyeh and black cord. In his hands was a wooden rake, him reaching to the highest branches for the olives up there.

It was an odd moment to my American sensibilities, what felt for a moment like a kind of intrusion: a public garden, its trees being harvested by a bedraggled family for what had to be personal use. Or maybe they'd been hired to do this, to gather up the olives and deliver them to some press somewhere. The whole family at it, these ancient blankets beneath meant to catch whatever bounty they might find, those old plastic crates here to carry it all in once the olives had been gathered by the kids.

They were Bedouins, the poorest of the poor. The outsiders. Though citizens of Israel, they had no access to services provided by the nation—to electricity, to water, to telephones and gas and sewage—because they lived in desert camps and not in permanent villages where those services could be found. Instead they were still nomads, their homes small tent cities surrounded by broken-down trucks and cars, rusted barrels and plastic bins and other gathered debris, their sheep pens cordoned off with fences made of old dead branches.

So yes, I realized, my smugness broken down in just that moment in Bloomfield Garden. Please do this. Please harvest.

Now, here, the woman shook her stick in the branches. The man, balanced on the top step of the ladder, combed through its boughs somewhere up in there. Here their children waited.

And I could see, each one caught in the headlights like small stones, the quick scattered fall of olives.

No one honked, and I suddenly understood the beautiful way, the tender-hearted way this traffic jam comported itself, the sweet Sabra finally manifest.

Here was the living out in big city Jerusalem what God had commanded in Leviticus, about not reaping to the very edges of your field or gathering the gleanings of your harvest, that instruction to leave them for the poor and for the foreigner residing among you happening here, right here.

"I am the Lord your God," that verse in Leviticus ends.

No one honked. Instead, we each of us thoughtfully, carefully—quietly—maneuvered around the outside edge of those sheets and quilts laid out on the street, each lane allowing the next car through. All of it silent, and respectful, and tender as traffic around a family and an olive tree could ever be.

Nothing *balagan* here.

What to Drink: Tea

PLENTY OF FRIENDS CAME to visit while we lived in Jerusalem, giving us more than enough reason to see pretty much all the holy sites in Israel. But in January, once our dear friends Jeff and Hart from Charleston had spent the week touring all things Jerusalem, we decided to take a quick trip out of Israel and go see Petra, the ancient city carved into sandstone canyons, over in Jordan.

Things were complicated getting there: first the five-hour drive down to Eilat on the Red Sea, the day bright blue and very cold, the road long and lonesome from Jerusalem east to the Dead Sea, then straight south. All the while, and as ever, the land could have been the desert between Los Angeles and Las Vegas. Except this was Israel. Not just Israel, but *Old Testament* Israel: We passed, halfway down and beside the very end of the turquoise Dead Sea, a rather large rock formation called Lot's Wife that did, in its way, and at the right angle, resemble a woman looking back. She stood at the base of Mount Sodom.

This was Old Testament Israel.

Then, two hours of desert farther south, here arrived the startling surprise of the deep blue Red Sea. Deep *deep* blue, and beautiful.

Beside it sat sharp square eruptions of white resort hotels and restaurants: the resort town of Eilat. Sailboats, miniscule triangles, cut along on the wind on that dumbfoundingly blue water; brown desert mountains on both sides of the bay cupped the city and the water and those boats out there all in their hands. On down the right side of the bay lay Egypt, to the left Jordan, Saudi Arabia a couple miles farther down that coast. Four countries in one grand view.

Next came the border crossing at Aqaba, the Jordanian resort town settled beside Eilat. Fewer hotels, but still right there on the beach. But to get into Jordan and so to Petra, there was the border to cross. No rented

Israeli cars can enter Jordan, and so we parked in a small lot set up just for this purpose. As per standard operating tourist procedure, we'd arranged to have a taxi waiting for us on the other side for the rest of the drive—two more hours—up to Wadi Musa, the town at the entrance to the slot canyon into Petra.

The border buildings looked more like an outdoor carwash and bus station in that same California/Nevada desert than an international border between two countries known for the wars between them. Metal awnings atop poles, a kind of long and low and narrow building with different sets of windows, each with its cut-out passway for sliding through a passport. From there we walked another hundred yards or so between passport control on the Israel side to the same set of buildings on the Jordan side, each of us toting a duffel as we walked the rough macadam road between countries. We were the only ones there, January the off-off-off season for this sort of thing.

Once through Jordan passport control, we saw a taxi in the parking lot, a man leaned against the hood. He'd emailed us a picture of himself—Aref was his name, a slightly older man with salt and pepper hair and a thick gray moustache—and once introductions had been made all around, Aref gracious and smiling as he loaded our duffels into the trunk, we piled into the car, me in the front seat, the rest in the back. Aref started the engine, and Arabic music came on the radio: oud, violin, a drum and tambourine, what sounded like a flute and another stringed instrument. The oud was the only one I knew the name for, mandolin-like and with a big belly. Above it all the thin high nasal voice of the singer.

More California desert, but now we were in Jordan, headed up through a craggy pass and into higher desert, then up onto the King's Highway, a blue road sign right there out my window proclaiming as such: *King's Highway* in English, above it words in Arabic, I could only assume, for the same.

Here we were, on that route Moses walked when he led the whole nation toward home. Here we were, right here, in a taxi and driving it!

But it was a long ride, and we were tired, and we were hungry. Conversation lulled, Aref still with the radio on, most all the songs very much alike, and so, just to fill the car with words, to make small talk with this man we'd spent so long with already, I asked him, "What is this song about?"

He smiled, nodded, his eyes to the road, to the radio, to the road. "Okay," he said, and nodded. Then he set about listening, and nodding, listening, nodding, all while the high-pitched voice tremoloing on. Finally, he nodded hard once, and said, "There is this boy." He nodded along again, listening, then nodded hard once more. "He loves this girl," he said, and went on listening, nodding, listening. Then he smiled, gave that hard nod one more time, and said, "But she does not love him."

He glanced at me, slowly nodded: There's what this song is about.

We all burst out laughing, and I turned to Jeff in the back seat, said, "Country music is everywhere." Aref laughed as well—he knew American country music too, said "Johnny Cash!" right then—all of us heading higher and higher on the King's Highway, up toward Petra.

We arrived after dark in Wadi Rum and checked into the hotel at the entrance to Petra, then spent the next day, just as cold and sun-drenched as the one before, hiking the bright and towering red stone ghosts of the ancient city. We hiked, and hiked, surrounded all day long by tombs and monuments, temples and edifices, pillars and staircases and homes and an amphitheater too, all carved into brilliant red sandstone, and brilliant mauve, brilliant magenta and beige and brown and cinnabar and cochineal sandstone all just as brilliant in this sun, and in this cold.

But the next morning there came a snowstorm, unheralded, a surprise, and we found ourselves snowbound in Aref's taxi at the crest of the King's Highway only halfway to Aqaba, elevation 5,000 feet, hours and hours and hours from Jerusalem.

Aref had assured us before we left, light snow falling on us as he loaded our duffels into the trunk out front of the hotel, that the snow was no hazard, that we would be safe. "We can make it," he said, smiling, but in it a kind of tension, a kind of vague qualm: the ends of his moustache went up for the smile, but his eyes showed none of it. And so we left, the radio off, only to drive into light snow that turned into heavier snow that turned into a blizzard, the cab slowing and slowing and slowing until it mired fully in the snow.

Aref turned to us then, no smile to his face, and said, "We cannot make it."

He called in to report what had happened and assured all would be well, all would be well, and forty-five minutes later members of the Jordanian Army—yes, the Jordanian Army—emerged from the white all around us, men in drab green heavy jackets at our snowed-over windows. They'd driven their emergency response truck as close as they could to us, then hiked the rest of the way up the King's Highway to the taxi.

We were relieved.

Jeff and I helped the soldiers push the taxi out of its fix, and as soon as we'd rocked it free Aref pulled away and drove off—he couldn't park and wait for us to climb back in, because we'd get stuck in the snow again, of course.

That left Jeff, me, and five soldiers to walk a mile or so through a blizzard back to their rescue truck. Along the way we pitched snowball fights, America versus Jordan. I actually yelled that out as I reared back to launch a snowball, and was nailed in the shoulder before I could even let go. All of us were laughing, talking—they all spoke perfect English, one of them a Michigan grad—while we tried our best not to think of the cold.

Then here was the rescue truck, emergency yellow, sharp and big with its pug-faced grill and running boards two feet above the snow-packed road. We all climbed into the warm quad-cab, the driver inside and ready to go. Eight of us jammed inside a cab meant for six, Jeff and I in the back seat in the middle, a soldier on either side of us.

We were in, settled, we eight talking and joshing, ready to find our taxi somewhere on the road back toward Petra. But now one of the men in the front seat pulled from the floorboard a battered Thermos, and another soldier up there produced from somewhere a stack of four thick glass tumblers. The one with the Thermos unscrewed the lid, and poured out steaming hot amber tea into first one glass, then another, both held by the one who'd brought out the tumblers, who then handed them back to Jeff, and to me. The first two glasses of hot tea in the midst of a blizzard we were all suffering through.

I don't even like tea, but I cannot remember tasting anything as perfect as that sweet and strong hot tea, its steam immediately clouding over my glasses. Amber tea sweet beyond sweet, yet not staggeringly so: a jet blast of warm sugar tempered by the earth of the tea and the cool lip of the glass it had been poured into.

That was when Jeff, glass in hand, turned to me and said, laughing, "This is going to be a great story."

"Yes it will," I said.

Pink Peonies and the Western Wall

ONE DAY WHEN I was maybe thirteen or fourteen—we were living in Phoenix then—my mom brought home from the Basha's grocery store a bag of bagels. They came in a clear plastic sleeve, six of them, though most of the sleeve was taken up with the big fat letters of the brand: Lender's. Though I'd heard the word "bagel" before, I really had no clue what they were. Round, I could see, and thick. Sort of like a hamburger bun but with that hole in the middle. She'd also brought home a bar of Philadelphia cream cheese, a strange silver ingot that took up residence along with the bagels in the refrigerator.

She let we four kids know they were there, and told us too that when she was a girl she used to have toasted bagels and cream cheese together. Not too long after that she started bringing home pastrami from the Basha's deli, and rye bread, and a little later Hebrew National hot dogs, the kind that popped when you bit into them.

My mom was a cook of her time, most all her recipes from made-for-the-American-housewife magazines: beefaroni, chicken and dumplings, lasagna, though made with cottage cheese and meat sauce out of a jar. She made fried wontons filled with sausage and green onions and garlic, monkey bread and cheesecake, Jell-O salads and garlic cheese grits and baked cheese potatoes. And there was her notorious Milky Way cake, with its six melted Milky Way bars as part of the batter.

She was a good cook, and we ate, and we were thankful.

But to this day, I really don't know what happened to her when I was in my early teens, and she started bringing home these new food items. The only thing I can say with any certainty is that there was now this food—Jewish food—showing up in our fridge.

And it was good.

She grew up in Hollywood in the forties and fifties, and the stories I'd heard of her having toasted bagels were from when she was a girl sitting in Schwab's Pharmacy on Sunset, where my bit-actor grandfather had taken a job as a busboy because of course Lana Turner had been discovered at the soda fountain there, and he wanted to be discovered too. Turns out Lana getting discovered there never happened (it was at the Top Hat Café a couple miles farther up Sunset). And my grandpa, Thurston Earl Holmes, never got discovered. Anywhere.

He was a narcissist, but one of the fun kind, a practical joker whose antics—turning up the radio in the car as loud as it went just as you, the kid beside him, were about to nod off, or elaborately sneezing into a hand-kerchief only to pull it open to show a wad of mayonnaise he'd put there before—were always designed to make him and his wit and his laugh the center of all.

But even more than a joker, he was a storyteller, the grandiose tales of his Hollywood escapades legion. He claimed to have been a stuntman in *Magnificent Obsession* (he said he was the floppy-hatted Confederate soldier chasing the beloved goose out front of the farmhouse), and in *Red River* too, and that he knew John Wayne and Howard Hawkes both because of it. He said he knew Eve Arden, and Lucille Ball, and Walter Brennan too.

And he told us time and time again of how he played cards regularly with Clifton Webb and Howard Hughes. Once a week.

My grandfather's agency information sheet from 1964—he had an agent, and was a member of the Screen Actors Guild—read, "Thurston has 30 years of radio and screen credits. He made his motion picture debut in the 1933 production of *West Point of the Air* with Wallace Beery. In all, he has appeared in over 75 feature films. From radio parts in the various Hollywood based shows to the present TV productions, he has been seen in over 40 TV shows including his role as Dr. Harvey on *The Andy Griffith Show*. Artistic floral arrangement is Thurston's hobby. He also rides well and enjoys participation in all sports."

But if you look up Thurston Holmes on IMDB, you'll find him listed only once, and not as Dr. Harvey on *The Andy Griffith Show*, but as Charlie in the episode "Mr. McBeevee," though the credits that appear at the end of the episode itself list him as "Lineman."

How tenuous a television credit is *that*?

In the episode, he's the stunt double for Mr. McBeevee, a telephone lineman who befriends Opie one day, but who neither Andy nor Barney believes is real because of Opie's description of him as having a silver hat and that he walks in the trees (this episode is one of the all-time fan favorites, I might add). When you watch it, there's a couple shots of Mr. McBeevee up on a telephone pole all geared up and climbing down, and I can tell by the way he moves that yes, that's my grandpa.

And if while you're on IMDB you look up *Earl* Holmes, the other name he used, you'll find the two other credits he's given: One as a Western Union Boy in *Swingin' Along*, a goofball comedy starring a very early Barbara Eden and a pre-*Hollywood Squares* Peter Marshall. In it my grandpa has two lines—it took some sleuthing to find a copy of this classic—when he hands over the telegram to Peter Marshall's mother; one of those lines is meant to be funny, but he couldn't have delivered it more flatly, and I remember thinking the first time I saw the scene, sadly, wistfully, it's no wonder he never made it.

The other listing is as a Confederate Soldier in *13 Fighting Men*, starring Brad Dexter just before he makes his star turn in *The Magnificent Seven* as Harry Luck, the one of the seven no one can actually remember. But in this one my grandpa delivers only one line, yet he does a surprisingly good job of it. The Civil War has just ended, and a group of rebels is going to steal a shipment of gold heading for Union troops. When the captain—Dexter—tells his unit they'll be killing the soldiers for the gold, my grandfather stands and says he won't have anything to do with killing anymore, and deserts the unit. It is a laudatory decision; it is a memorable moment in film history; it is an utterly forgettable movie. And my grandpa has exited stage left eight minutes in.

So how did he end up playing cards with Clifton Webb? And, of all Hollywood people, Howard Hughes? Once a week?

What was the truth? What was lore? Myth? Legend?

And what does this have to do with Jewish food?

This: My mom told us her own stories of growing up in Hollywood in the shadow of my grandpa (and my grandma too, a character larger than life herself who'd been a singer for a very brief time in Kay Kyser's big band, and who cussed like a sailor, smoked like a chimney, and sang like a dream; she was also pretty much blind from glaucoma my entire memory of her, though she never missed a tip of the ash off her cigarette into the beanbag tray she kept with her at the dining room table in their mid-century rancher in Pacoima out in the San Fernando Valley, where she'd sit singing to herself all day long and play solitaire, the deck of cards with outsized numbers and symbols she had to hold right up to her eyes, her winning nearly every game she played—but I digress).

My mom told us of how she dated Carl Switzer—Alfalfa from the old Spanky and Our Gang movies—when she was a teenager and he was 27, the date set up by my grandpa who knew Switzer from the Hollywood Masonic Lodge he'd joined because John Wayne and Gene Autry and Roy Rogers were members there. She told us too that Switzer was an arrogant jerk. She also told of how when she was a girl she took trapeze lessons in the grand back yard of one of her school chums, the yard replete with a safety net and plenty of room to work. Another childhood playmate was a boy named Lincoln who could play the piano unbelievably well—Oh, the two of them were such good friends!—and then the boy grew up to become Lincoln Mayorga the composer and arranger, writing and contributing to the soundtracks for everything from *Chinatown* to *Pete's Dragon*—he even arranged the original "Dirty Water" by The Standells and "Tainted Love" by Gloria Jones—then ended up giving classical piano concerts at Carnegie Hall and with the Moscow Philharmonic. In Moscow.

My mom told us that when she was in junior high in Culver City she sat and watched from the second story classroom windows cheap westerns being filmed in the studio lots across the street; she claimed that when she was in high school Dean Stockwell took her roller skating; she was supposed to be cast as one of the baby munchkin Sleepyheads who wake up in their nest and rub their eyes at the news the Wicked Witch is dead in *The Wizard of Oz*.

But the strangest story we heard growing up—and here's where the whole matter of Jewish food ties into this long digression into Hollywood Tall Tales—was of when she was served cold beef tongue at the home of the mother of Jay Sandrich, the television director.

It's a story that was told to us so many times we children could repeat it word for word. When she was a little girl, the three of them went to Mrs. Sandrich's house in Beverly Hills—she was so very nice, and had such a lovely house!—where she served them sliced meat that looked like a tongue, then she was told it *was* tongue, and she nearly threw up at the news. But she was polite and ate the serving she'd been given, the meat so chewy she didn't think she could swallow it, only to have the nice lady heap seconds onto her plate when she saw how much my mom seemed to love it. And my mom ate that serving too.

It was a scary story when we were kids, the idea of eating a *tongue* of all things; my mom shuddered every time she came to that word *tongue* in the telling of the story, and laughed when she told of getting a second helping by that nice lady.

Later, once I'd grown older and figured out who the heck this Jay Sandrich was, the story seemed even stranger, one I could never make sense of: Jay Sandrich is the beyond-important director and producer of such utter classics as *The Mary Tyler Moore Show, The Golden Girls, Get Smart,* and *The Bob Newhart Show.* Every time we watched any of these programs on television and his name showed up during the credits, my mom called out "That's him! That's Mrs. Sandrich's son!" and she'd tell us the story again.

Years later, still bothered by this story—or perplexed might be a better word—I'd do my research and find out his father, Mark Sandrich, the nice woman's husband no less, was a truly iconic Hollywood figure, directing five of the Fred Astaire-Ginger Rogers classics, including *Top Hat* and *Shall We Dance,* as well as the ultra-classic *Holiday Inn* before dying of a heart attack in 1946.

But, I have always wondered, how the heck did they get into her house in Beverly Hills for this Jewish of all Jewish meals? How did they know the widowed wife of a Hollywood legend? My grandfather was the ne'er-do-well actor, the busboy at Schwab's, waiting to be discovered. They were always poor, living apartment building to apartment building, where they shared the bathroom at the end of the hall with the other tenants. They wouldn't own a house until my mom was in high school. And my grandfather would never be discovered.

And how—this is the really strange part—did my mom end up with an oil painting of peonies in a blue vase, in the lower left corner the pale green signature "Sandrich"?

Because that was always the end of the story my mom would tell: Mrs. Sandrich, at the end of this luncheon in her home in Beverly Hills, gave my mom a painting of hers.

My mom had it hanging in our house as long as I could remember there being things on the walls. A painting of pink flowers, a blue vase, that name.

And along with it a story of beef tongue.

Later, me grown up and married and gone, beginning the life of a writer with reasons to be in New York, my Jewish food touchstones became the pastrami monoliths at Carnegie Deli and the cheesecake slabs at

Lindy's. On trips into Manhattan to see my agent and publishers over the years, Melanie and I made our regular pilgrimages to Zabar's, where we bought rugelach and bagels, their babka with its lovely chocolate striations through the bread. For several years we had monthly shipments of their coffee along with the baked goodies sent down here to South Carolina. We ate bagels—the chewy kind, not those fluffy imposters you can get in any grocery store and, well, in most bagel chains too—with our cream cheese and the exotic add-ons of lox and red onions and capers, though I must here confess it's Melanie and our two boys who love lox, and not me. I'll just have the red onions and capers with a good thick shmear of chive and onion cream cheese, please.

Somehow, somewhere, in different places and with different friends and acquaintances, we'd end up having matzo ball soup now and again, and of course the ongoing pleasure of hot pastrami and corned beef, and latkes might make a cameo appearance too. Five or six times a year at the College of Charleston, students in the Jewish Studies Program bake and sell challah for anyone on campus, and I became such a regular that Enid, the admin for the department, sent me emails with the memo line THEY BAKED CHALLAH AGAIN! and always saved me a loaf.

But all of this is simply lining up a row of food items we knew and loved. Things to eat, and to enjoy, though sometimes those student-baked challahs were a little dry, and funkily braided, but hey, these were students just trying to raise money. There was nothing in our minds or on our palates of the history of the bagel, its Ashkenazi beginnings in Krakow in the 1600s when the word *bagel* first appears (though there's a recipe in the Renaissance chef Bartolomeo Scappi's world-changing 1570 cookbook *Opera dell'arte del cucinare* for *ciambelle*, dough rounds made with eggs and flour and goat milk and rosewater, that are first boiled and then baked—but again, I digress); the fact the word rugelach means "little twists" in Yiddish wasn't in our consciousness, or that pastrami migrated here in the late 1800s with Jews from Romania, where the traditional brining process results in a cured meat, no matter what cut or animal, called *pastramă* (a *păstra*: to preserve), and that the Romanian Jews, these new Americans, started calling it pastrami in order to let it rhyme with the already-popular cured meat they saw for sale everywhere: salami.

We had no idea the word *challah* is Hebrew for loaf.

Who knew? We didn't. This was just good food.

When my mom and Jacob came to stay with us for much of December when we lived in Jerusalem, only five months had passed since my dad had died in Sequim, the town out on the Olympic Peninsula they'd retired to five years before. His death was sudden, though not, finally, a surprise. He'd had diabetes for the prior twenty years, and was in the hospital in Port Angeles to have his left leg removed, and died of a gastric ulcer the night before the surgery.

The fifty years before he'd retired had been spent in Southern California, where my father worked for RC Cola, save for that stint from 1967 to 1974 when we lived in Phoenix, my dad transferred there to run the bottling plant and the sales force. My mom held our home together all along, and once we got to Phoenix she also took on jobs: at that Basha's grocery store where she'd bought that first bag of bagels and brought it home; later, at one bank, then another. Once back in California—Huntington Beach— she stayed working.

And making beefaroni, chicken and dumplings. Fried wontons and Milky Way cake.

Not long after Melanie and I had settled into our apartment in German Colony, my three siblings and I agreed that maybe a trip to the Holy Land might help her as she navigated her new life inside the grief she'd been delivered now that he was gone.

Jacob had a girlfriend back then who seemed to dictate much of his life, even to the point of how he wore his hair: thick and tousled on top so that long curls fell down over his forehead (even Jacob confessed to us at one point that trip that he didn't like his hair this way). His clothing consisted of a pair of jeans and those aftermarket sweatshirts and T-shirts— Sparco, HKS, Greddy.

My mom flew from Seattle to JFK, where she met Jacob, who'd flown up from Charleston, and together flew overnight to Tel Aviv, where we met them that morning in that warehouse of a reception hall at the airport, with its low semi-circular wall a hundred feet from the opaque glass doors that whooshed open every time someone came out from baggage. Around us was the same gaggle of friends and family and flowers and balloons as every time we came here. But this time we were the ones waiting for the arrival of someone else. Our own loved ones.

Then here emerged Jacob with that hair and the Sparco sweatshirt, in either hand a suitcase handle to coax the rolling bags along—one his, one his grandma's—and beside him my mom in a black sweater and pale blue blouse, her green leather purse that seemed to carry everything in the world crooked at her elbow.

Looking as bleary as anyone would ever look. She'd flown over twenty hours to get here, though once we'd all hugged and I'd taken one of the bags from Jacob, she was as happy and talkative and freshly lipsticked as ever. But her hair was also smushed to one side, her eyes seemed to have a hard time staying open, and she was leaning on Jacob and walking very slowly, her arm linked in his as we headed outside and into the cool December morning.

She was seventy-one. Her husband had died only five months before. She'd flown all this way. Her hair was smushed—an incredible lapse in protocol for her, but an understandable one all the same.

My mom was beautiful. Her parents were both beautiful too, her dad that bit actor, her mom that one-time big band singer. No wonder she would inherit those good looks.

But as her son I never knew it. Once, when I was a senior in high school and the wind ensemble held a concert at the high school gym, she came up front before we started just to say hello, to wish me luck. I played first chair alto saxophone, Dawn Bergdahl, one of our two drum majors during marching band season, beside me in second chair. My mom shot the breeze a little with us, and I remember feeling a bit embarrassed. Yes, there was a general pre-concert hubbub going on and it seemed no one paid any particular attention to us—the concert wouldn't start for a few more minutes—but this was my *mom* hanging around, small-talking. I don't remember being mean or brusque to her, but I do remember suffering through a low-grade mortification the whole while.

When finally she left, I let out a breath, shook my head for the benefit of Dawn, who would certainly understand how I'd feel about my mom up here talking to us. But when I turned and looked at her, her mouth was open, her eyebrows high on her forehead, her eyes on my mom walking away. She blinked, then looked at me. "Is that your *mother*?" she said.

"Yep," I said, and shook my head again.

Her eyes were back on my mom, then on me. "She's *beautiful*," she said, the word long and drawn out.

What? I remember thinking, and looked out into the audience to see my mom heading down the middle aisle toward wherever she and my dad were sitting.

My *mom*? Beautiful?

I thought about it a moment, and realized that, well, yes. She was beautiful.

And still she was, there in the reception hall in Israel, a country I couldn't imagine ever going to, let alone living there, back when I was in high school. But here she was. And here too was our son, a strange and wonderful gearhead even more unimaginable than the idea of living in Israel way back when. A son!

He was tired too, I could see. Like his grandma, he was blinking a lot, working to keep his eyes as wide open as he could.

So what did we do, once we'd driven them up to Jerusalem, gotten them fed (bagels from Tal Bagel just up the street), unpacked and showered?

We ran them ragged.

Over the next twelve days we'd go to the Western Wall at sunset for prayers; Bethlehem for that strange gantlet-running of a trip to see the Church of the Nativity; Nazareth and the Church of the Annunciation, built over the cave where Mary lived when Gabriel appeared to her—a moving and majestic place, with its rough-hewn rock grotto surrounded by high walls and stained glass; the ruins of Capernaum with its glass and steel chapel hovering over the stone walls of the room where Jesus healed Peter's mother-in-law, the sick lining up at the door that evening; Be'er Sheva to hear me give a lecture to a group of Israeli teachers of English at the university there, where ten minutes into my keynote speech one of the conference directors came up on the dais and handed me a slip of paper upon which was written "Please finish"; Beit She'an and its ruins of colonnaded streets and exquisitely detailed mosaic floors, its vast Roman baths; Tel Megiddo—in Greek, Armageddon—in the Jezreel Valley, the hill upon which cities had existed for thousands of years but across which a trench had been plowed like a slice through the middle of a cake by archeologists in the early twentieth century; Caesarea and the promontory of Herod's Palace, the rocky shoreline with its vast rectangular pool, foundation stones of the rooms around it leading out into the bright blue Mediterranean, this the exact place where Paul defined and defended the faith, first to Felix, then to Festus and King Agrippa and Bernice, none of whom saw any reason why Paul should be imprisoned. But it was from here, this edge of the world, that Paul left for Rome for his appeal to Caesar.

All this, and more.

Here's how much we ran them: The Tuesday after they arrived was my teaching day at Bar-Ilan, and we'd arranged for Mickey, our erstwhile guide, to take Melanie and Jacob and my mom on the day-tour of all the important sites in Jerusalem: the Tomb of the Holy Sepulcher, the Mount of Olives, the Garden of Gethsemane, the *suk*, the Via Dolorosa. All of it.

When I got home that night from work, the apartment was dark, no sign of anyone. They'd started this morning at nine and were supposed to finish up before five, and here it was five-thirty already, completely dark outside. I started to worry, stepped out of the apartment and peered down our cul-de-sac to busy Emek Refaim for any sign of their arrival. But there was only evening traffic out there, beyond it Café Hillel lit up, people inside bundled against the cold and ordering, as ever and always, their *hafuchs*.

I stepped inside, worried now, and paced a minute or two, and then here they all came through the door, Melanie and Jacob and Mom, cold and tired.

"Well," Melanie said, and started in unbuttoning her coat. She let out a breath, said, "We did it all."

I told them I had been worried, wondered where they were, and then said to my mom, "So did you see Jesus' tomb today?"

"Oh," my mom said, shrugging off her jacket and slowly shaking her head, "we saw so many tombs today I know it had to be one of them."

That's how much we put them through.

Even to that first day they arrived, a day we should maybe have called quits after the walk we took up and down Emek Refaim, where we stopped to admire the cellophane-wrapped trays of pomegranate seeds in the produce bins out front of the little grocery store we always went to—Pomegranate seeds already out of the fruit! What a luxury!—and stopped for an American-style coffee at The Coffee Mill, the cramped and keenly aromatic little shop with one whole wall of coffee bean bins, exotics from around the world.

But no. That wasn't enough for us to do that first day. Because we had plans.

That night we were bringing them to a real live Shabbat dinner in the real live Jewish Quarter of the real live Old City.

One of my colleagues in the creative writing program at Bar-Ilan was the novelist and story writer Allen Hoffman (one of my favorite books is his collection *Kagan's Superfecta*, each story a word-feast at once grandly intelligent, laugh-out-loud funny, and deeply moving), and one afternoon in the hallway outside the Department of English I mentioned to him my son and mother's upcoming visit. He's a funny man, tall and gray-haired and kippah-wearing (his was black velvet), and always with this wry kind of smile, as though he's assessing the punchline of what could be a funny joke.

"Bring them over for Shabbat dinner next week," he said, and shrugged, put his hands out to either side. "What else can you do on a Friday night in Jerusalem?"

And so I took him up on it, not thinking about how they'd only be arriving that day, and that we'd get home from the airport a little after noon, and that by the time they got showered and fed it would be after 1:30, and how sunset—when Shabbat began and we were supposed to arrive at the Hoffmans'—would be at 4:37.

A little after four, we drove from the apartment up Emek Refaim and onto the road that wound around the base of Mt. Zion—what should have been a ten-minute drive but which took twenty for the Friday evening traffic—and pulled into what was then the parking lot outside the south walls of the Temple Mount, a place where now an entire palace complex lies unearthed and is still in the midst of being explored. Not just any palace, either, but Solomon's Palace, and its surrounding streets, markets, homes. But this evening it was only a skim of asphalt atop it all, white stripes painted to delineate where to park.

On the way there I'd coached—maybe lectured is the better word, though browbeat is a contender too—Jacob and my mom about how we had to be careful to watch, and listen, and follow the directions we'd no doubt be given about how to partake in a Shabbat dinner. This was a holy event, and there were rules, protocols, sequences, all that. We were guests being allowed to participate, and needed to pay attention to what was going on in order to best pay our respects to the traditions central to this evening's meal.

I went on too long, yes, even though I'd never been to a Shabbat dinner myself. But this was important, Allen's invitation a genuine gift, and we could all respect that, right? Sure!

We walked into the Old City through the unfortunately named Dung Gate, the gate closest to the parking lot and also closest to the Western Wall. Dung Gate, where garbage and, yes, dung had been traditionally dumped outside the walls, was a smaller entrance into the city than Jaffa Gate, maybe only wide enough to fit a good-sized car through the crenellated limestone wall, and the street was massed with people. But we just pressed into the throng, me first, Melanie holding my hand, then my mom holding hers, Jacob following up at the rear, his grandma's hand in his.

Just inside the gate lay a bank of turnstiles we passed through, scores of soldiers watching us all spill through them and out onto the limestone plaza, the high Western Wall to the right and dotted with its tufts of hyssop growing between cracks.

The plaza was already filled, people visiting and singing and dancing in huge exuberant circles all over, everyone delighted. Shabbat had come, and with it the ordained day of rest.

This was Kaballat Shabbat, the Friday prayers, and the highlight of the week. The plaza gently sloped down toward the Wall itself, where people prayed, the area below the Wall partitioned, women on the right, men on the left. From where we stood a hundred yards away we could see down there the sea of black fedoras and fur shtreimels and simple kippahs bobbing up and down, the men in prayer, and saw too the women in their shawls all together and praying.

It was, like the other Shabbat evenings we'd been to here, a holy party. People sang, people danced, people talked with each other, smiled, wore flowers, carried books, talked with each other even more. And smiled.

We'd be taking my mom and Jacob there for prayers soon enough, but right now we were already late. Allen would be meeting us out on the plaza opposite the Wall, where stone buildings three and four stories tall looked down on this all. Apartments, yeshivas, offices, some with narrow lancet windows, some with vast picture windows, some just ordinary predictable glass squares, but all of them with a view onto this most holy of sites in Judaism, punctuated every Friday at sunset by this vast and happy shindig celebrating the presence of God.

I hurried us through the crowd toward the buildings, to their left the public stairs, wide stone flights that led up from the plaza and into the Jewish Quarter up there. People poured down them and into the plaza to join the bash already going on, we four swimming against the stream, until there stood Allen at the bottom. It was cold that evening, but he only wore his customary blue oxford shirt and khakis, and of course that black velvet kippah. He'd told me when we'd set up the dinner we'd never find their apartment in the maze of alleys and sidestreets and covered passageways that made up so much of the Old City, and so to look for him at the bottom of the stairs, and now here he was, smiling and nodding and waving us over. After shouted introductions of my mom and Jacob—he'd already met Melanie any number of times—we started up the stairs, still with its cascade of God-minded revelers pouring down upon us.

We followed him up flight after flight, stopping now and again to take in the view of the plaza down there, swarming with sound and joy, those circles of people dancing like wreathy wheels turning in place, and still people passed us headed down these stairs.

Once at the top, Allen careful to keep a pace that accommodated my mom while entertaining us with stories of living in the Old City, its difficulties and blessings, we turned right onto a street, doorways into the stone walls beside us. Small stone planters sat out front of them, and in the dying light I could make out rosemary and sage and thyme; windowboxes high on the walls held dormant geraniums that would in a couple months become bright blasts of red and orange and purple. Then we turned onto another narrower street, those stone walls and their doors even closer, the street itself sloping up and up, and then we stepped into a covered alleyway that curved up and to the left, its ceiling arched stone. We were in near dark now save for the small lamps on the walls outside the doors every few yards up the alleyway, and then Allen stopped at one on the right, said, "Here we are," and opened the door, led us in.

His wife Steffi, smiling and sweet, brown-haired and with glasses, ushered us into a cozy—really, this is the word that comes to me as I write this, *cozy* in its best sense—apartment, before us a front room with a sitting area to the left and just a little crowded with a sofa and chairs and maybe one side table too many, to the right a dining room table all set, beyond that a doorway into a brightly lit room that had to be the kitchen.

But the smell—the *aroma*—was what welcomed us before a single word had passed between us. A warm smell: a little bit sweet, a little bit herbed, calm and welcoming. A smell like home.

We made introductions again, and met Allen's mom who was there to visit. Immediately she and my mom were talking, while Allen took our coats and headed off into a darkened room past the sitting area, then came right back out to where connections were already being made: Allen was from St. Louis, the city where my mom had been born, and they were off. Jacob smiled and nodded, polite and unafraid to engage—he'd put on a black sweater and khakis for this, the aftermarket garb set aside for the event.

But it was apparent, even inside the pleasantries, that things had to get going. We'd been late because of the crowd at Dung Gate, and in the plaza, and though no one said anything about our timing, I knew sunset was long gone, Shabbat begun.

The table was set with a white tablecloth, napkins, dishes and plates, wine glasses and utensils all perfectly placed, at the center two candles already burning. We'd missed the lighting of them by Steffi, done just before sunset to begin the Shabbat proper. At the head, the far end of the table closest to the doorway into the darkened room, stood an open bottle of wine and a silver cup, beside it what looked like an embroidered black handkerchief with white fringe over a small heap, this on top of a small wooden board—a cutting board, it looked like, beside it a bread knife.

Allen took his place up there with the wine and cutting board, and he and Steffi helped us decide where we'd sit, Melanie and I placed on one side, our backs to the entryway to the kitchen, across from us Allen's mom, then my mom, Jacob, Steffi at the foot of the table, opposite Allen.

But we didn't sit. Instead we stood behind our chairs, and Allen said, "We start with singing Shalom Aleichem," smiling and nodding at us, these newcomers to the whole thing. "It's a poem that welcomes in the angels to Shabbat dinner and asks for their blessings of peace on us, and you're just going to have to bear with us because it goes on for a while and my singing voice just isn't what it used to be."

We all gave a laugh, and he and Steffi and his mother began singing what felt a long song that seemed to repeat itself a great deal. His eyes were up, toward heaven, I figured, and there were words I thought I could pick out—*Shalom* a few times, and *Baruch*, what I knew meant Blessing—and I kept my eyes on him, watching, fearful he might glance down at me to find my eyes wandering the room while still they sang.

Then they finished, and next Allen told us the Shabbat dinner itself began with reciting the verses in Genesis about the first Shabbat, and started right in singing in Hebrew by himself. The first few words were low and quiet, but the rest—maybe thirty seconds or so—a little louder, and I was able to pick out from the rush of sound the word *Elohim* a couple times before he was finished. Next he asked each of us to pass up our wineglasses, where he poured out a bit from the bottle beside that heap with its fringed cover. He passed back each glass, all the while narrating that the wine represented the bounty of God's blessing, and the celebration reminds us of the Exodus from Egypt. Shabbat is a happy occasion, and so wine celebrates the day and God's gift from the land. He poured wine into the silver cup then, held it with two hands, the bottom of the cup sitting on the palm of one hand, the other holding it by the brim. "Now the Kiddush," he said, and launched into the Hebrew blessing of the wine.

I finally let myself glance around then, smiling all the while. Jacob glanced at me but without a smile, my mom beside him watching Allen, her face serious—her mouth will go thin when she's paying particular attention, and she'll tilt her head just a little. Steffi and Allen's mom both were nodding at the words Allen spoke, watching him.

And suddenly the smile on my face made me feel a little like a tourist, a little like a faker, a little like I was too carried away with the novelty of this, and the fact we were showing my mom and my son a real live Shabbat dinner in this exotic locale we were living in, and I understood already, at just this beginning of the evening, that there was something else afoot beyond the kind of floor show I'd made this become.

Of course this was important. But I'd let the event eclipse the meaning, me too worked up about the act of it, and not its purpose.

There was a ritual happening here, and a blessing. There were thousands of years of history—thousands—being played out in these few words Allen was saying in a language I didn't understand, and thousands of years of history in the wine inside this glass I held, and in the glasses my son and my wife and my mother held too.

All this in the pouring forth of words from Allen, him singing. *Baruch* I picked up again, and *Adonai*, the song ending with the words *hah Shabbat*, and *Amen*.

Then Allen sang a few more short lines, his eyes on Steffi, who nodded along, smiling. When he finished, he glanced around at the rest of us, said, "That's the Eshet Heyil. The verses at the end of Proverbs where the woman of valor is given her tribute. So Steffi, we salute you!" and he nodded to her, smiling.

"Allen," she said, and shook her head.

Here we were, on the Sabbath, celebrating it in Jerusalem.

"L'chaim," Allen said, and brought the cup up, and we all toasted one another, sipped at the wine. I looked at Mom, who didn't like wine, but was known to partake of the occasional margarita or mimosa. But the cup was to her lips, and she looked at me a moment, and I could see was smiling even in that sip.

"Next we wash our hands," Allen said, and sort of bowed with a hand out toward the kitchen behind Melanie and me, "but first the rules."

I'd already started to turn, but stopped, the only movement at the table Steffi and Allen's mom who were already heading in. "One last thing," Allen said. "We can't say anything once you've washed your hands until we bless the challah. So just rinse and dry, then come back to the table and have a seat. Then, after we bless the challah and each of us takes a bite, we can talk again." He shrugged, still with that wince and smile. "Sorry about all these regulations, but nobody ever said it was easy being Jewish. We're God's obsessive people."

We laughed—even Jacob let out a kind of *huh* at the joke—then headed into the kitchen, where Steffi and her mom were already drying their hands on a cloth set beside the sink.

The kitchen was small, counters and sink to the right, to the left the stove and fridge and more counters, three crock pots beside the stove.

And foil everywhere.

Foil covered the counters. All of them. Foil lay over the stovetop so that the rings themselves weren't visible, across one side of the stovetop a glass baking dish, covered in foil. The knobs on the stove were covered as well, the foil draped off the front edge of the stove to cover the controls. Even the crockpots had been lined with foil, their control knobs covered with crimped slips of foil too.

Foil everywhere: bright, expansive. An aluminum kitchen. I'd never seen anything like this, and I turned to Steffi, all of us crowded in now to this small space, and said, "This is amazing! Why—"

She shook her head before I could finish the question—*Why all this foil?*—her eyebrows up, a kind of closed-mouth smile on her face, and I could see loud and clear exactly what she was saying: *Weren't you even listening? I washed my hands already!* She shrugged, in the move a friendly *Oy vey!* tossed in for good measure.

"Oh," I said, "oh," and she smiled, shook her head again, put her hand out to the sink: *No worries. Just wash your hands already. We have a whole dinner to eat.*

I nodded, nodded again, in me the awkwardness of my stupidity, the thickness of my embarrassment.

Beside the sink sat a large green plastic pitcher, and Allen's mom, standing just past Steffi, nodded at me, touched the pitcher and motioned for me to pour it out, and I finally got it. By this time Allen was chuckling at the end of the line and I glanced up at him, saw his smile. "Welcome to Shabbat charades," he said. "Pour some water from the pitcher over your hands, then use the towel there to dry off. And quit with the small talk."

Jacob was slowly shaking his head, a very solid smirk on his face, his dad's folly a gift, and Melanie, beside me, smirked too, while my mom just took in the kitchen and all this foil.

We all washed our hands, dried them, then trooped in silence back to the table. By now Steffi and her mom had taken their seats, signaling us we should sit too, and when Allen, last, sat down, he lifted that black fringed handkerchief off the heap on the cutting board in front of him to reveal, finally, two flawless loaves of challah, perfectly braided, golden and shiny, and of course why hadn't I figured out that was what lay there? Challah! Shabbat dinner!

Allen said, "This is *Hamotzi*, the blessing of the bread," and lifted the two loaves up in front of him, and sang again, a brief line this time, once more inside it *Baruch*, and *Adonai*. He set the loaves back on the cutting board, then pinched up something from a small bowl up there, sprinkled it over the bread. "Salt," he said, and picked up the bread knife, started slicing. He spoke of how the bread was the symbol of God's provision while the Jewish nation was in the desert, the manna found each day and gathered by the people for food; two loaves on Shabbat dinner reminds us of how God provided a double portion of manna the day before Shabbat. As he passed to each of us a piece of the challah, he spoke of the salt, and how the temple sacrifices at the altar required it, and once we all had a slice, he looked at us, smiled, nodded, and we picked up our slices and took a bite.

What is there to say but that there was a moment of wonder to the flavor here on my tongue? The crust with its simple tear, the bread soft and yeasty and sweet, that bit of salt popping in as I chewed to bring up the pitch of flavor, its timbre, to something like life, something like peace.

"So," Allen said then, "let's eat!" and though Steffi and her mom stood just then, made for the kitchen, and even though both Melanie and my mom made to stand too so that they might help and were sweetly shooed back down by them both, I only tore off another piece of this challah—this life—and ate it, then took another, and another, the slice happily finished in a matter of moments.

We ate.

First, matzo ball soup. We each were presented with a bowl of clear and golden broth, in it bits of carrot and celery and onions, small shreds of chicken too, at its center a single round dumpling the size of a small egg, glistening and pale. I could see traces of dill in the broth and atop the matzo ball, and leaned forward, took in a deep breath of the subtle fragrance—there was garlic in there, too, along with that dill—while Steffi and her mother took their seats. I waited a moment, as did Melanie and Jacob and Mom, all of us glancing at each other, hands still in our laps, all of us wondering what next ritual might be called for before we could dig in, this warm and steaming soup wafting its promise like a temptation.

Then Steffi took her spoon, sliced down into the matzo ball, and took a bite. Our signal to start.

I first took a sip of the broth—perfectly salted and chicken-rich, which is to say not watery but filled with the quiet blend of the vegetables and that dill and the touch of garlic, and of course that chicken, and then I too sliced into the matzo ball, took my first bite.

Light, seethed in that broth but not heavy with it, a texture simple and full and bread-like, and puzzling for the way in which this texture and this taste of the broth yielded a third element: a feeling of home, of being where one ought to be when with family on a cold December evening just after sunset. Where one should be on a Sabbath.

I scooped another slip of the matzo ball with my spoon, a smaller one than the first, me already rueful at the fact this would be finished soon, and that manners—blasted manners!—would keep me from asking for another bowl.

A general hubbub arose from we guests, all of us—even Jacob—as we kicked in about how delicious this was, and Steffi smiled, shrugged, humble and happy. She explained then, in answer to my dumbly-timed question, that the foil was everywhere because Shabbat food all has to be cooked before sunset and then kept warm but not directly on the heat. That would constitute cooking, and so it would be considered work, the foil on the stove and in the crock pots serving as a kind of barrier between the heat doing that work, and the food simply being kept warm. The foil on the counters everywhere was just to make sure all the food stayed clean for Shabbat.

I was impressed.

Next came serving dishes, one with herb and lemon-baked chicken pieces, another filled with *tzimmes* (pronounced tzim-mess; I had to check the spelling too), a kind of casserolly stew of carrots and sweet potatoes and prunes and honey and orange juice and spices all baked for a couple hours. There were bowls of Israeli salad, and a green salad too, and crispy potato kugel, each serving like a slab of deep-dish hash browns, and more and more and more of that challah.

We talked, Allen holding court over the proceedings with his wise cracks and smile. We talked about flying from the States, more about St. Louis, about how we'd be covering every square inch of the country the next couple weeks, about Jordan and our plans to visit Petra, about growing up in California, about the car horn being as utilized a tool in Jerusalem as the gas pedal, about the best place in German Colony to get rugelach and baklava and every other pastry you could think of, a place down an alley and hidden away, no sign out front. Simply a place you had to know about.

We talked too about Shabbat, and the prayers, and the goings-on we'd seen down there on the plaza, those circles of people dancing, the singing, and Allen, handing me yet another slice of challah, said, "You can actually see the Wall from the terrace off the bedroom," and pointed over his shoulder toward the darkened room behind him.

And of course I, in my impetuous stupidity—right in line with asking a question of a person I'd just been told couldn't speak—said, "Really? Can we go see?"

Allen blinked, his eyes straightaway to Steffi at the end of the table opposite him. He shrugged at her, dipped his head to one side a moment. He was quiet, his eyes back on me, then to Steffi, then to me, and the silence among us seemed to stretch a very long time. "Sure," he said, and started to stand.

"Never mind," I said, and "I'm sorry," though for what I couldn't say. Just that I'd taken some misstep and knew right then I'd breached protocol with the request. I'd asked, I already knew, for something that meant a regulation broken.

So much for my browbeating the family on our way here.

"It's all right," he said. "We're supposed to stay seated until the Shabbat dinner is over, but it's okay. You didn't know," and he was already standing in the doorway, the room dark behind him, and waving us all in. "God is merciful, and I think He'll forgive us if we go take a look."

I stood, and then Melanie, who looked at me, slowly shook her head: *You boob.* Jacob shook his head too as he stood: *I am in full agreement with my mother's assessment of you.* But my mom, who seemed a little perplexed about what was going on, only looked at Steffi and Allen's mom, said, "Are you coming too?" to which they both replied, "No," and smiled. Then she stood, still a little confused, and we all headed for the doorway.

"I'm sorry," I said, following Allen. In the darkness I could see a bed to the left, on it our coats, ahead of us another open doorway, just past it what looked like curtains in front of a sliding glass window.

"Stop with the kvetching already," he said, "and be careful in here. We didn't set the lights before sunset so we can't turn anything on, so pay attention you don't trip," and now we were in a smaller room, a washing machine in the dark to the right, to the left shelves and baskets. He pulled back the curtains right in front of him, slid open the glass door, and stepped outside. He held the curtains back for me to take, and I stepped outside too, turned the curtain-holding over to Melanie, and likewise until my mom and Jacob were out here with us.

It was a small corner terrace, hip-high stone walls in front of us and on the right. There were a few other buildings higher than this, but we were, for the most part, at the roofline, before us gray domed roofs and gray flat roofs and other gray terraces, all crowded in amongst each other.

Allen stood right in the corner of the terrace, where the walls came together, and I could see him leaning to his right a degree or two over the wall. "It takes a little bit of work," he said, "but you can see it if you stand right here." He stepped away, and I moved in, leaned just the smallest bit to the right, just as he'd done.

And there, a few hundred yards away and wedged between two domed roofs, lay a shard of bright beige, a wedge of the Wall lit up and dotted with pinpoints of hyssop. Maybe two inches wide from here. But the Wall, all the same.

"There it is," Melanie said from behind me, and I looked over my shoulder, saw she was leaning out too, and Allen said, "It's tough to make it out in daylight, but at night it's right there."

I moved away to let in my mom then, who edged up to the corner. "Where is it?" she said, peering off without leaning, and I said, "Just lean to the right a little. It's between two domes." She leaned right then, but too far, still looked for it, her head moving back and forth, until Jacob, just behind her, lifted his arm and leaned in close to her and pointed. "Right there," he said, his arm and finger a track she might take in order to find it.

"Oh," she said, "I see it!" and Allen said, "Not much to shout about, the view of it. But that's the Wall."

"Oh," my mom said again. "It's beautiful!"

Once we'd returned to the table, Steffi and Allen's mom sitting there, smiling, waiting, and once I'd apologized yet again, and again, and one more time for the breach I'd caused, we finished dinner, dessert and coffee brought out to us next. Honey cake, moist and sweet, pound cake-like and with the little twist of earthiness only honey can give. We talked more, about the Department of English, about what it was like to grocery shop and live in the Old City, about the tourists that had to be taken into account every time you walked out your front door.

Just people—one an observance-breaching fool—at the end of a fine dinner, talking, sharing, being together.

When finally we were done, Steffi and Allen's mom cleared the dishes, while Allen got up and went to one of the side tables in the sitting area beside us, pulled out little blue pamphlets, and came back to the table, gave us each one. "One last blessing," he said, and took his place at the head, Steffi and his mother back from the kitchen and settling in. "This is the Birkat Hamazon, the blessing after the meal when we give thanks for all the blessings we've received, and ask for blessings too, on the family, on Jerusalem, on all the Jewish people, on everything. The English translation runs right alongside the Hebrew so you can read along." He opened his booklet, held it with both hands, and we all did the same, and I glanced at my mom, her eyelids as heavy as I would ever see them, trying to keep them open.

The pamphlets were worn, the covers a little tatty, the page edges a little frayed. They'd been around a while, and for a moment I wondered how many times they'd been used, and realized immediately the ridiculousness of such a question: every Shabbat. Every Friday sunset at which thanks were given for the blessings received, and the blessings needed. Even to this night, here, this my own family's moment to give God our blessings and to seek them from Him too on a Shabbat evening in Jerusalem.

"This is going to be a long one, so hold on," he said, and began to sing, he and his wife and his mother.

We listened, and were blessed.

We didn't talk much on the short ride home. The plaza had pretty much emptied, the parking lot thinned out. Allen had walked us from the apartment to the top of the stairs, made sure we knew where we were going from there—down and to the plaza, then right to the turnstiles and out the gate. Only a ten-minute ride, but by the time we pulled off Emek Refaim into our cul-de-sac, Mom was already asleep.

Once in a while through the years after I'd ask her what she remembered about visiting with us, if she recalled that quip about seeing so many tombs that one of them had to belong to Jesus. She didn't remember that, or the dinner at the Hoffmans' either.

But she remembered taking off her shoes and socks and stepping up to her ankles into the Dead Sea, and doing the same in the Mediterranean there beside Herod's Palace in Caesarea. And she remembered sitting beside Jacob on the long flight from JFK to Tel Aviv, her grandson keeping her company through that night.

Now and again she'd still tell the story of beef tongue and Mrs. Sandrich, and sometimes that date with Alfalfa, until even those memories disappeared as she slipped into Alzheimer's, and in 2019 she passed away.

The last time I saw her, in August before she died in October, she had no idea who I was, though she was still sweet, smiling and chatting away with me and with Melanie and my little brother Timmy, we three strangers sitting with her in the TV room at the memory care facility in Sequim. Then, in the middle of our visit and apropos of nothing, Mom leaned forward in her seat on the sofa beside me, and said, "But I do have a surprise for you," and in the same moment reached into her purse and snapped out a blue and white plastic hand clapper, waved it at us, the hands slapping loud and sharp. We three jumped for it, and she burst out laughing, the daughter of her practical joker father still here with us.

On the clear blue day of her funeral, twenty-seven of us, all family, gathered graveside in the cemetery out on the Olympic Peninsula where my father had been buried thirteen years before. The cliffside tract of land overlooked the Strait of Juan de Fuca, the sky so keen that morning it seemed we could reach out and touch Canada just across the water.

We stood at her gravesite, and told stories about her, we siblings and husbands and wives and grandchildren, and when it came my turn, I told of discovering she was beautiful only when Dawn Bergdahl pointed it out before that concert back in high school, and told the story too of being with her that last time a couple months before, and how she'd pulled out that clapper, scared us all but made us laugh. Melanie and I had gone to a Family Dollar store in Sequim the day before and bought a plastic hand clapper of our own, my intent in telling the story at the funeral to do just as she did and pull it out at the exact right moment, snapping it around to surprise and make laugh the entire gathered family.

But just as I tried to pull the clapper from inside the breast pocket of my jacket, it hung up in there, and I was left to struggle to get it out, the whole moment lost.

And yet the story of my mom and my failed practical joke still had a happy ending. After the service I gave the clapper to my youngest grandchild, two-year-old Noelle, daughter of now-grown-up Jacob and his wife Sarah. Noelle had been especially delighted when I'd waved it around, however ill-timed and however close to this grave, and now as I held her on my hip and she slapped it again and again, laughing, happy, this toy became a piece of the story of her great-grandmother, and a piece of Noelle's own story too.

After the funeral, we three generations came together to celebrate her with her food. All twenty-seven of us gathered into a house in Sequim, there to eat, and remember.

What we ate were all the best dishes she used to prepare for us, all from the recipe cards she kept, safely held by our sister as our mother slowly passed away. The heirloom dishes: fried wontons filled with sausage and green onions and garlic, monkey bread and cheesecake, a Jell-O salad and garlic cheese grits and baked cheese potatoes. Her notorious Milky Way cake, made by Melanie, with its six melted Milky Way bars as part of the batter. A spiral cut honey-baked ham, Mom's favorite, was the only store-bought dish.

We ate. Three generations feasting from the provision of words on recipe cards, penned by my mother. The ongoing stories that made up her life had ended, but the familiar and comforting and brand-new-this-moment tastes of her food remained alive in us all.

And in this manner, with our partaking of the blessing of her food, we were all partaking in a ritual thousands of years old, as old as gathering families together to share a meal of an evening and doing so in remembrance, the meal and our gathering a celebration of blessings.

I call my sister, Leslie, out in California a couple times a month, and she calls me, and we talk about everything. Lately, though, it's been about how little we knew of our mom, and how little we can know of anyone. How once one dies, the stories are gone, and there's no way to ask what was real, or made up, or a melding of both.

Leslie remembers that story my mom told about the friend with a trapeze in her backyard, and about her roller skating with Dean Stockwell, and I remember the stories about watching cheap westerns being filmed from her junior high classroom, and the bagels, and that beef tongue. But each time we talk, we come to the same fact: she's gone, and so our chances to have asked her what was true and what wasn't are gone now too.

But here's another fact, as true as the fact her stories are gone: A couple years after my father died, Lincoln Mayorga was going to be in concert in Los Angeles, and my mom wrote to him. He wrote her back immediately, and the two went out on what, for lack of any better term, were a few "dates," spending time sharing stories of when they were just kids growing up in Hollywood all those years ago.

And another: One afternoon when we were kids and at my grandpa and grandma's house out in Pacoima, my grandpa rattled around in the garage and found a small reel of film, then set up his sixteen millimeter projector and roll-up screen for us right there. He fed the film edge through the labyrinth of gears, had one of us cut the lights there in the garage, and started the projector.

There, soundless on the screen, came my grandpa bursting through the front doors into Andy Griffith's jailhouse office, Andy sitting at his desk, Barney perched on the edge of it and talking. My grandpa wears a white fedora with a black band, and what looks a white suit, a black tie, and he tears to the desk in a fluster.

In his hand is a black leather doctor's bag.

"I was Doc Harvey," he said, "and the whole episode was about how the doctor was out of town while everyone got sick, and now at the end of the show he finally shows up." I remember looking at him then, his eyes on the screen, and seeing two of him—this one here in the garage older, the one up there on the screen younger. "This is the little joke piece just before the credits," he went on, "but they cut it because the episode went long."

So he really *was* Dr. Harvey, just like his agency info sheet proclaimed back in 1964.

But where that piece of film—that proof—has gone, I will never know. It resides now only in my memory, and is testified to on the agency's faded piece of paper I keep in my desk.

And I've tried to contact Jay Sandrich through his agency three times since I began to write this in order to find out if in fact his mother was a painter, and in the habit of giving away her work to little girls over for a lunch of beef tongue. But there's been no response, and I can only imagine what some email-answering intern at the office in Hollywood, already jaded and world-weary, might think reading a letter from someone asking as obtuse a question as mine, though I've attached a photo of the painting each time, evidence of something someone once painted and signed in pale green letters "Sandrich."

My sister still has it, one of the few things my mom had left when she died. A painting of pink peonies in a blue vase. Proof—if we believe it, and we do—of a lunch of beef tongue, and a second serving because she politely finished the first.

Treif

WE WANTED BACON. We needed it. We had to have it.

So I asked around. Across the cul-de-sac from our apartment was an American family who'd moved here a few years back in anticipation—like a number of people we'd met—of Christ's imminent return. Sweet people, though it seemed to us in the two or three times we talked they might be a little anxious, a little too earnest: the toll of bet-hedging on who might lay eyes on Him first, when all Christ told us was to be prepared, and to have our wicks trimmed and enough oil. To be on the alert, because He had no clue Himself when He'd be back.

But our neighbors knew of no place we might buy bacon.

I asked a few people in the department at Bar-Ilan who lived, like us, in Jerusalem instead of Tel Aviv, fully aware of the deep breach it might be to ask after how I might break kashrut—the ancient dietary laws within the Jewish tradition—and in so doing asking them to aid and abet in my transgression. I asked my grad students too who were always eager to help the ever-stranger in this strange land. One of them had heard of a butcher in Tel Aviv somewhere, another had heard a rumor of one up in Netanya. But these were miles—many miles—from where we lived.

All we wanted was to wake up of a morning and make some eggs and bacon, just like the old days. Just like back home. Yes, we'd accompany them with a good sturdy bagel nothing like we could get back home, and some of that Bulgarian cream cheese we'd never even heard of before landing here. But the bacon would make us feel more like being home.

Still I got nothing.

And still we wanted bacon.

Not until we were at Linda and Donald's for dinner one night and had pled our case to them both were we rewarded with the news of our good fortune.

"Oh yeah," Linda said there at the table, our plates empty now, wine glasses nearly so, we four pushed back from the table, sated as only we could be after one of Linda's extraordinary meals. "There's one right here on Emek Refaim. It's a tiny place, right around the corner."

"Maybe a hundred yards from your apartment," Donald put in. He chuckled, slowly shook his head. "Of course if we're ever asked if we were the ones to send you there, we will neither confirm nor deny." Donald. The observant attorney.

I found it the next day. A tiny place, as predicted, not a hundred yards from our apartment, right here on Emek Refaim. We'd passed it a hundred times on our way to somewhere else—Linda and Donald's, Doron Falafel, Burgers Bar, Joy, the grocers, the post office, the bakery. We passed it every time we walked up to Bloomfield Garden at the end of the street, where we came to look out on the old city.

But it was an easy place to miss. Nestled in amongst the happy and colorful and bustling restaurants and boutiques, the store was merely a whitewashed front with a wide glass window. No signage. Just a lonely storefront, while beside it on either side bustled happy commerce.

I stood on the sidewalk out front of it a little longer than I would have otherwise. It looked forlorn, sad. It was, in its own way, a little intimidating, and maybe even wrong. Maybe the carnivore equivalent of a porn store. They sold meat in there unblessed by the Rabbinate.

They sold bacon in there.

I pushed the glass door open, stepped inside.

Havoc: a man in a black fedora and black suit, strands of his *tzitzit* visible beneath the bottom of his vest, stood yelling in Hebrew, a fist in the air and shaking at a thin man with black hair behind a glass meat case between them. The thin man wore a white short-sleeved dress shirt, I could see, the glass meat case chest high. And he—the butcher, had to be—was yelling right back.

I very nearly left the place, ready to let the glass door fall closed in front of me. But such was my need for bacon that I withstood this unexpected high drama—very high drama—and stepped in.

They continued. And I saw then that the man in black held in the other hand, the one not in a fist and shaking, a white plastic grocery sack. In it a weighted something. A package. Product.

Meat.

The meat case stood on the right wall, the product inside it covered loosely in pieces of white butcher paper. On the left wall were shelves of spices, jars of pickled goods, the walls all white. At the end of the shop, straight ahead, was a cash register, beside it two slicing machines, the kind in every deli. Beyond it all was the back room with a butcherblock table, long and wide, past it two doors on industrial refrigerators. On the table lay a very large hunk of meat.

They yelled.

I nosed along the shelves, pretending what was going on wasn't going on, and then the man in black moved to the door in two decisive steps and turned, raised that fist again. Next came a vast and what seemed complex pronouncement, most likely, I figured even as he was speaking it, a curse of Shakespearean proportions, if not Biblical. He pushed the glass door open and stalked out—exit stage left—the white plastic grocery sack with its product tight in hand.

I looked at the butcher, who let his eyes linger at the door a moment, then put his hands on his hips and looked at the floor. He slowly shook his head, let out a hard sigh, and moved from behind the meat case to the machines, that register. He didn't look at me, said nothing, and now I could see he had on an apron tied at the waist, the cloth stained in the way only a butcher's apron can be stained, the lower part of his shirt stained too.

He crossed his arms, seemed to sway just the smallest bit. He shrugged, shook his head again, all with his eyes to the floor.

"So what was that all about?" I said, because there was an empty space in the room, and because sometimes I talk just to fill the air. Sometimes—ask Melanie—I just ask people questions, no matter how appropriate or not they might be. Just to break the ice.

And because I am curious. Nosy, actually.

He let out a breath, put his hands on his hips, and said, his voice near a whisper, "The price."

I am not making this up.

"Oh," I said. "Oh." Irony rang through the air, replacing the emptiness from only a moment before. Irony too thick even now to examine. But irony.

He glanced up at me, his chin down, then looked back at the floor. Almost begrudgingly, as though perhaps the words he might say next were a kind of burden, a weight perhaps he could not bear, he said, "May I help you?" his voice still in that whisper, the words slow, thick with an Arabic accent.

"Oh," I said. "Bacon," I said. I tried at a smile, though he still wasn't looking at me, then stepped to the meat case. The butcher moved along with me on the other side, and reached in at the end closest to the front of the store, pulled back a sheet of the white paper, to reveal a slab of bacon. Thick, fatty, beautiful.

"I enjoy this meat," the butcher said, his words barely audible, still just as slow, and he reached in, lifted the beautiful porcine gift from the case. He stood, and seemed then to give the smallest smile, his eyes on the bacon.

In this way our friendship began.

I was in there once every week or so from then on, and never saw another customer. There was always only me and the butcher, him in that stained white shirt and apron, his voice never changing from that whisper. When he'd yelled at the customer my first time in, his voice had been full, solid, but after that I found myself having to ask him to repeat himself time and again. And even though his end of our conversations usually consisted of one or two sentences three to five words long, there was something in him that let me know he enjoyed—or at least appeared to enjoy—when I came in. He'd give that slight smile, sometimes actually let his eyes meet mine, then pull back the paper covering the bacon, in the move a kind of humble bravado: *Voila!*

Slowly, over weeks, I found out he lived outside Jerusalem, up beyond French Hill to the north, and had a cousin in Dearborn, though he himself had never been to the States. He was a Christian, and had a wife and kid, and enjoyed his job. His father had been a butcher, and the business had been around for nearly fifty years, though never in a monumental way. Just a business.

The meat case also held chicken and beef and lamb and more pork. Sausages—sausages!—and butts and shoulders, steaks and shanks and chops, all cut to portion. Product waxed and waned in the meat case, so I knew there were other customers who made it in. But all I could imagine was that they waited for the coast to clear before entering this *treif* of all *treif* locales. They wanted no witnesses.

Treif—like always, there's a smorgasbord of alternate spellings: *trayf, trafe, traif*—is a Yiddish word, grown from the Hebrew for torn, *teref*, and refers to the mauled carcass the Hebrew nation was forbidden to eat in Exodus.

Eating a torn animal made one unclean, while eating one butchered by *shechita*—the blessed practice of slaughtering an animal as humanely as possible—was just fine.

So long as the animal had a divided hoof and chewed the cud. Which left out the pig and its magic: Give it corn or apples or swill to eat, and it gives back bacon.

There are plenty of ideas about why God disallowed a good many of His creations to be eaten by His chosen people back when Moses first received the Law from within the swirling cloud up on Mt. Sinai. In 1178, Maimonides, perhaps the most influential Jewish philosopher and Torah scholar (not to mention personal physician to Saladin), wrote *The Guide for the Perplexed*, a delightfully and practically titled book attempting to bring religion and reason together. Of this subject—why some food was acceptable and some wasn't—he observed that some sages believed this and other puzzling ordinances were simply tests of obedience to God's will. Either you obeyed and passed, or you disobeyed and failed. Others, he noted, held that God's reasons stretch beyond our own and therefore can't be questioned, but that there was a reason in there somewhere. It just isn't in we humans to figure out the reason of God.

But Maimonides didn't sit on any fence about the food, and held specifically that, when it came to things nonkosher, it was all about health. "I maintain," he wrote, "that the food which is forbidden by the Law is unwholesome." And pork came in for a particular slapdown: "The principal reason why the Law forbids swine's flesh is to be found in the circumstance that its habits and its food are very dirty and loathsome. . . . A saying of our Sages declares: 'The mouth of a swine is as dirty as dung itself.'"

Agreed. But I am thankful every day—and not just for the fact I can eat bacon—that God, in His glory and mercy, saw to it that Peter had his vision on the rooftop of Simon the tanner's house in Joppa, when three times in a row something like a sheet filled with "all kinds of animals and reptiles and birds of the air" descended from the sky. With it each time a voice commanding him to take and eat, a command Peter declines, only to be followed up with that same voice declaring, "What God has made clean, do not call common."

Then, in the perfection of God's timing, the two servants and the soldier dispatched by Cornelius the centurion up in Caesarea, a God-fearing Gentile who has received his own vision from God, arrives at Simon the tanner's, there to bring Peter to Cornelius to hear what he has to say.

It's a request unheard of, a monumentally nonkosher thing to do: a Jew coming into the house of a Gentile. Peter is already with the unclean, staying at a tanner's house, a profession considered so chronically unclean—all that daily touching of dead animals—that even the Mishnah, the first written gathering of the Oral Torah, directs that tanneries, like the dead, be outside of a city, and downwind too. ("Animal carcasses, graves, and tanneries must be distanced fifty cubits from a town. A tannery may be set up only to the east of a town.") But this notion of entering a Gentile's house was even worse.

But the Gospel, of course, is what God had given Peter to say, and with it, once he and the gang head back up the coast to Caesarea and Cornelius's house, arrives salvation to the Gentile world.

Cornelius: my direct ancestor in the church. The first wild olive shoot grafted into the true tree. Because of him, and because of Peter's vision, and because of God's grace, I was allowed to enter into God's presence. I was made whole.

One day in November Melanie and I decided to ask Jackie and Derek over for dinner, our first guests to the apartment. They'd both been of such great help from the start and that first visit when I'd taught in the program with the American Center the year before. When we arrived here to live, they'd had us over to their apartment for dinner the first week.

Jackie and Derek. Yes. Our first guests.

But what would we serve?

We were, in our way and on this first occasion of having guests to dinner in Jerusalem, paralyzed by kashrut, afraid we might offend with serving up something we shouldn't. People here had entirely separate sets of dishes and pots and pans and silverware, one set for dairy meals, one for meat. We'd even seen kitchens with two refrigerators, two sinks, two ovens and two dishwashers.

What were we getting into?

The only way around our not making a misstep, we finally realized, was simply to go to Jackie and ask what we might cook for them. We'd never done such before, never invited someone to dinner and asked them to set the menu. But we were on new ground here. We were the guests in this house, as it were, asking the owners over.

Jackie surprised us utterly: Make a southern dinner for us. As southern as you want.

Really? I asked, because a Southern dinner means pork. It means ribs. It means, to my way of thinking, baby back ribs, barbequed.

Pork.

Please! Jackie said. We'd love it. We wouldn't dare be offended. We're you're guests. It will be delightful to have a meal we never get here.

What a relief. We could do this. We could.

I went to the butcher's the next day. Each time I went in I still looked to see who might be watching. Was that couple at the café table across the street staring? Was the woman pushing the stroller rolling it particularly wide of me? Were these two boys in their kippahs side-eyeing me as they passed, me alone outside this plain white storefront? It always seemed so. But I had business to attend to. A friend to visit.

He'd have to order them.

Immediately upon my request—he knew what they were, baby back ribs, of course he knew what they were—he'd put his hands on his hips, said, "This will take some time." He stood behind the counter, crossed his arms, put a hand to his chin, looked at the ground. "I will order. But will take time." He turned, took a step and another and another, tapped his chin with his finger as he walked: a man already on a mission.

Then he stopped. "Week and a half. I will get these to you." He stopped, turned to me.

He was smiling. Then he nodded, slowly.

We set the rest of the menu. Along with the ribs, we'd have my mom's garlic cheese grits, a nice green salad, biscuits. Nothing over the top, not too many dishes. Keep it simple.

Dessert would be brownies and ice cream, our household default. Sure, brownies weren't really Southern—there exists in certain circles to this day a simmering dispute over their origins as being late 1890s to early 1900s Chicago, Boston, or Bangor, Maine—but they're a decidedly American dish all the same. They would do.

We'd brought grits with us, believe it or not. I'd grown up with them— of course I did, my father from Mississippi, my mom's stock from east Texas—and Melanie, from Southern California with a few years in New Jersey but who, sadly, had never had them before meeting me, had grown used to the idea of serving them alongside scrambled eggs and bacon for breakfast, and the treat of my mom's garlic cheese grits now and again as a side at dinner.

Garlic cheese grits. Yeah.

The green salad would be easy: iceberg lettuce and onions, tomatoes and red peppers. A quick vinaigrette. The biscuits would be homemade, though we'd found Bisquick at the grocers just around the corner. But that would be cheating and, finally, I've never been a big fan. There's always just too much of a metallic taste to the goods you can make with the stuff, a grain or three too heavy on the sodium aluminum phosphate in with the baking powder. These biscuits had to be good—we'd be representing a whole food culture on this evening of Free-From-Kashrut dining. Biscuits mattered.

There was the issue we'd have to muscle through of measurements we'd found online for the biscuits, the American recipes all in teaspoons and cups when what we had at hand in the kitchen were metric equivalents. But the BBQ sauce was easy, a golden South Carolina sauce that flowed from its yellow mustard source like a spring of tart and sweet and a little hot happiness. Definitely not that red stuff you could buy anywhere, even in Jerusalem. As ever, it would be just a gathering of the usual eyeballed ingredients: yellow mustard, brown sugar, a little ketchup, Worcestershire sauce, apple cider vinegar, cayenne pepper and paprika and salt and pepper and a touch of garlic and onion powder. Don't forget the cayenne. The cayenne.

And there was the matter of where—and how—to actually barbeque the ribs themselves. Our Arab apartment was small to begin with, and had no kind of patio to it outside. Only steps up from the street itself, four of them, beside the steps on one side a kind of low limestone wall maybe a foot wide that stood only as tall as the four steps up to the door, so that the wall at its top was flush with the doorsill.

Maybe, I thought, I could balance a barbeque there.

But I had to get a barbeque too. A matter I hadn't even considered back when the idea of this dinner had suddenly struck. We have always had, and always will, a backyard barbeque, and a good two or three nights out of the week during summer it will be in use. The barbeque was a given in my way of thinking about a Southern dinner. It was a part of the landscape. It was the *there* to cooking in our house.

It all seemed so easy when Jackie had said to make us a Southern meal. Barbeque! Exactly!

I asked the butcher. If anyone might know where I could get some kind of grill, some kind of barbeque, some sort of outdoor setup I could park on a low wall and pull off baby back ribs, it sure seemed he would be the one.

He stood behind the counter, crossed his arms, put a hand to his chin, looked at the ground. He turned, took a step, tapped his chin as he walked.

Then he stopped. "Across street," he said. He turned to me. "In back of grocery store. Little barbeque you use one time."

He was smiling even bigger now than when he'd calculated how long it might take to get the ribs. He was engaged, I could see. He was *in*.

I turned and looked out the front window. From here I could see across Emek Refaim the grocery store where we bought the quick needs: milk, eggs, bottled water. And those cellophane-wrapped trays of pomegranate seeds already out of the fruit. It was a jam-packed store to say the least, and though not very big—maybe the size of a couple Circle Ks end to end back home—they carried everything, had a good produce section, a cheese kiosk, a bakery, wine and olive oil and meats and everything else. The aisles were narrow, maybe three feet wide, the shelves sky high. But they had everything in there.

Why not prepackaged one-use grills?

"In there?" I said, and turned back to him.

He nodded, slowly. "I think you will find one there."

He was *in*.

I found one stashed at the back of the store, stuffed in a bottom shelf cubby space with, of course, starter logs and matches and bags of charcoal. A little premade one-use barbeque, maybe twelve inches by twelve inches. A foil tray with snap-down metal legs, a grill, the charcoal already in there. Brightly packaged in red and black cardboard, on it a photo of swirling flames and a delectable piece of sauced chicken.

I stood there in the aisle and held the grill out in front of me, a kid at Christmas. Here was a grill to cook baby back ribs for my Israeli friends. I'd have to cut the ribs in smaller racks to try and fit them on there, and have to do a couple batches at that. We had two racks coming, enough, I figured, for all four of us.

This *treif* main might work after all.

Then I looked at the upper left corner of the cardboard packaging, saw a kind of printed crest. A stamp of approval, it looked like, writing in Hebrew and English both.

The grill was kosher.

Nothing went right at dinner. Only the salad and those Yankee brownies passed muster.

The biscuits came out flat. Maybe we'd messed up with the baking powder conversion, or maybe the kitchen was too hot when we mixed, the butter nowhere near as cold as it needed to be. We'd have been better off with Bisquick.

The grits—my mom's garlic cheese grits, my mom's famous garlic cheese grits—came out soupy, bled into puddles on the plates. The dish is meant more as a casserole than a pot of cooked grits, eggs used as a binder so that the final product is supposed to stand on its own. But my iteration bled. Mine puddled.

And the ribs. Granted, they agreeably fell off the bone when prodded with a fork, the slow-cook process foolproof. But when it came time to finish them off on the little one-use prepackaged barbeque, the heat just wouldn't come up enough to caramelize that South Carolina sauce. It might have been the cool of that November night, or the fact the layer of charcoal the tray came supplied with just wasn't deep enough. I tended the racks out there in the growing dark, the grill parked on that narrow limestone peninsula serving this night as my backyard barbeque showground, Jackie and Derek due any moment.

I messed with them. I turned them. I poked them. I covered them with foil to see if the heat might rise and retain, then figured that was stupid, that the moisture off the ribs trapped by the foil would end up just steaming them, then took off the foil and threw it away.

And still the heat wouldn't come up, and still no char magically appeared, no caramelization at all. They were, finally, wet though well-cooked baby back ribs, and when Jackie and Derek pulled up in front of the apartment, I'd had no choice but to pull them off, head inside, and serve our first two guests nothing like a fine Southern meal.

The salad was good. And Melanie, who'd long ago perfected the art of brownies, shone as the true artist this night. The brownies were perfect.

Jackie and Derek, the consummate guests—Jackie was, after all, employed by the State Department, and hence had storehouses of diplomatic skills from which to draw—claimed all meal long to enjoy the food, and seemed delighted with the ribs, those tender but merely wet and sticky testaments to the *treif* world from which this cuisine had sprung.

But the whole, finally, was a failure, despite the thanks and thanks and thanks.

The salad worked. And the brownies were good.

But there remains an extraordinary highlight to the entire doomed affair, one I keep close when running back through my memory of the night I failed Southern cuisine.

It came when I went to the butcher's to pick up the ribs. Two days before I even turned on the oven.

I stood outside the place the requisite moments spent looking to see who might be watching, then walked in. There were no other customers, only the butcher behind the counter. Without a word, he gave a small nod, then turned and went to one of the two refrigerators in the inner sanctum, pulled open the door. Then, like they were golden laurels, he carried the two racks out and laid them on the butcher block counter.

They were beautiful.

He stepped back and put his hands on his hips, gave a nod at them. He smiled, and met my eyes. "Here they are," he said.

I nodded too. These would do. Perfectly.

He weighed and wrapped them, in paper and then in a plastic sack, same as always. I paid him, and he handed them to me, but paused a moment, looking at me, the both of us for just that instant holding the ribs.

"How you prepare them?" he said.

It was a moment that surprised me, and made me feel happy and sorry at once. This butcher of very few words wanted to know how I would take care of this prize, this evidence of his skill, this confirmation of his vocation. But I hadn't even thought to tell him what the plan was. I realized, in the run-up to our first dinner, I'd only been after ribs.

He was proud of his job. He was proud of what he could do.

Maybe I'm putting too much on the moment. Maybe I'm seeing in the two of us holding these ribs, and his question right then, right then, just before finishing his end of the transaction, a value, a significance I am making more of than was there.

But I don't think so. I was there.

He was smiling. He wanted to know something from me.

And I had the best and easiest recipe ever for making fall-off-the-bone baby back ribs.

"Ahh," I said, and took the ribs then. I really said that: "Ahh." And with the package in hand—this *treif* bridge between us that crossed a chasm between cultures—I told him.

"It's my pastor's wife's recipe," I said, and I thought of her telling me this one day years ago on the sidewalk out front of the friends' house we were all helping move furniture out of in preparation for their heading onto the mission field. Two doctors, headed to Saudi.

"First thing," I started, "is to turn the oven up as high as it will go without turning it to broil. You just want it to be as hot as possible. Then you take the ribs, salt and pepper them, then double wrap them up tight in foil. Put them on a tray in the oven, and set the timer for twenty minutes."

I was enjoying this. I was giving the butcher—*my* butcher?—a preparation I'd done dozens of times through the years. I was warmed up here, excited, proud.

But the butcher had changed somehow. He'd lost the smile, his mouth a thin line. He'd closed his eyes. He'd put his hands on his hips.

I went on. "Then after twenty minutes you turn the oven off. Just turn it off, and leave it closed for two hours. Don't open it."

And now the butcher took on what looked a pained expression. His eyebrows came together the smallest way, wrinkles on his forehead.

What was happening here?

Still I went on. "After that, take them out and sauce them, then just grill them off." I shrugged, though he couldn't see that for his eyes closed. I smiled too, and of course he couldn't see that either.

"Easiest thing ever," I said, finished.

His eyes were closed. And then slowly, slowly he shook his head, his mouth still that straight line, his face in pain.

"What?" I said, maybe too loud. He was discounting the preparation. He was disapproving the whole thing. That was all I could think.

I'd failed him. The bridge had collapsed. That was all I could think.

"What's wrong with making it like this?" I said.

"No," he finally said, still slowly shaking his head. Then he whispered, "I am admiring."

That was the highlight—the success, the triumph—of the entire failed evening to come.

I won't ever forget that moment: the look on his face I'd thought was disapproval, but which was a kind of joy.

This story does not have a happy ending.

One day in December I went in for bacon. First thing I noticed was that one of the slicing machines was gone. The butcher leaned out into the passage between the counter and the backroom, nodded at me. He was on the phone, talking quickly, quietly, and turned away, kept talking, listening, talking. Then he finished, and came up front, rubbed his hands on his apron.

He was preoccupied, his moves a little sharper, a little quicker as he moved to the meat case.

"Bacon," I said.

"Yes," he said, and pulled back the paper covering the meat.

All he had was the end of a slab, a three-inch nub of sorts. Likewise with other meats in there: depleted. "This all I have," he said.

"I'll take it," I said.

He nodded, put it to the slicer set to the width he knew I liked—thick cut—and in a moment was finished.

"When will you have some more?" I said.

"Oh," he said, and glanced up at me as he wrapped the meat in paper, stuffed it in a plastic sack. "Not sure. Maybe not." He finished with the meat, set it on the counter.

"We are closing," he said.

We talked then. More than we had ever before.

He'd been on the phone to a butcher in Tel Aviv who was interested in buying the slicer he still had, the other one sold the week before to someone up north. He was in the middle of trying to get his brother to buy the meat case. The refrigerators might be bought at some point too.

They'd increased his rent. He'd been here all these years, but each year the rent went up, and now with the price of real estate in this stretch of German Colony—*the* stretch of German Colony, this posh neighborhood, this Soho of Jerusalem—he could no longer afford to be here.

Happy bustling commerce had pushed him out.

I told him how sorry I was. I told him I would miss the bacon, and him. I told him this was a good store, and that he'd helped us feel like we were close to home. We shook hands, and he nodded hard, once, though there came no smile.

The next time I went over, a day or two after Christmas, just to say goodbye one more time, the door was locked, the place empty.

I looked in that wide glass window, not caring if anyone out on the street were watching, sizing me up, side-eying me for staring into this *treif* home away from home.

The shelves on the left wall, those rows of spices and jars of pickled goods I'd nosed along that first visit, trying to ignore the high drama beside me, were cleared. The other slicer, up near where the register had been, was gone. The register too.

The meat case, empty, clean, still stood there.

And I realized I'd never even asked his name.

What to Drink: Lemon Mint Water

ANOTHER VISIT TO Israel. More readings, university talks, old friends, new students. More shawarma and falafel at Doron, more Bulgarian cream cheese and sesame bagels, more Israeli salad and Arabic coffee and good conversation and history and *balagan* traffic.

And another trip to Petra, this time only Melanie and me, and this time in May. No fears of a blizzard.

We start down the slot canyon—the *siq*—in the early morning, the high high cliffs striated reds and beiges and mauves and browns and more reds, the canyon a narrow gallery of curving walls like huge wind-danced sheets frozen in stone. Carved into the rock walls all the way in are water- and wind- and time-worn channels, man-made and millennia-old gutters that sluice rain down into the city, waist high on the right side walls, ankle high on the left. A feat of civic design set artfully inside the feat of natural design this canyon is.

Boys on donkeys trot back and forth past us, calling out with offers to give us and everyone else rides all the way to the Treasury; there are little carriages too, one donkey and two wheels and a single bench seat for three: a driver and two riders.

We walk the two kilometers through the *siq*, and we can feel the bit of altitude here—a little over 2,600 feet—because we live at sea level. But we take our time and pictures, pause and ponder, read all signage telling us what we see, because this is why we're here: to be here. Then, finally, we catch the first glimpse of the Treasury, revealed bit by bit ahead and above us between the shadowed walls of the canyon, a kind of shard-like flowering of sunlit orange, bit by bit, bit by bit, until the canyon walls open up onto a wide and open plaza surrounded by cliffs, and here we are.

On the far side stands the Treasury, massive, intricately carved, Corinthian columns and a broken pediment, figures up high, an urn up there too, all into the rock, and we have no choice but to think first-off of this same moment in *Indiana Jones and the Last Crusade* when Harrison Ford and company rush in on horseback to right here, right here, and this beautiful and huge and overwhelming and beautiful façade.

But it's only the start. We've walked a little over a mile, but there's still another mile and a half just to get to the base of the climb up to the Monastery. Then the climb up *to* the Monastery.

And so begins this parade of likewise carved façades: tombs, apartments, memorials, pillars, homes all climbing up the walls and the mountainsides, a wide dirt and gravel pathway through it all. People are amassing now, more and more tourists, those boys on their donkeys still riding through and calling out. A souvenir shop made of brick and wood and sheet metal for a roof sells refrigerator magnets and rocks and keffiyehs in all colors, out front of it several wooden benches to stop and rest and think about buying something. A couple of those boys with the donkeys sit on the rocks just past it, talking and taking a break of their own. Their two donkeys stand facing each other a few feet away, their reins in the boys' hands.

A small brown sign to the right of them points out the trail up to the High Place of Sacrifice. Stone steps lead up a canyon behind and to the right of the souvenir shop, and though we don't want to go all the way up there—we've read it's a couple hour hike—I'm thinking to head a little way into the canyon so I can turn around and get a photo of the wall opposite us, and all the façades there.

So Melanie and I start up these steps, carved straight into rock. Ancient, of course, worn low in the centers, but only steps, and we're just going up there a little way, just right up there to that rock where I can—

And I stumble, fall to one knee, only maybe a dozen or so steps up, and Melanie reaches out, holds my arm, and I hear shouted from behind me "Be careful!"

I'm up, I'm up—nobody panic—I'm up, and I turn to the voice, see those boys with the donkeys right down there, maybe twenty feet away. All the farther I've gotten.

They're still sitting, but are half turned to us, looking at us. One has on a ballcap, the other a red and white keffiyeh. They're both smiling at us, but they're both maybe fourteen or fifteen, so there's a kind of something else on the smile, a little bit of a teenage scoff: *Look at these tourists we have to deal with every day.*

Then the one in the keffiyeh turns a little more toward us. Still smiling, his eyes straight on mine, he calls out in the clearest English imaginable the most movie-worn line ever.

"*We need you alive!*" he calls out to me, then nods once, hard. More Harrison Ford than Harrison Ford has ever been.

We bust out laughing. How long has he waited to deliver that line just like he has? We laugh, and he and his friend laugh, slowly shake their heads, then turn back to their donkeys, go on talking just like they were before these tourists gave the one in the keffiyeh this perfect opportunity.

I forget to take a photo.

The walkway through this all widens and widens until the cliffs on either side give way to an even larger esplanade. To the left is an amphitheater the signage tells us can hold 4,000 people, the whole of it carved right into the rock. Signs point to more trails and sandstone staircases that lead away to points of interest, and the pathway empties into a broad kind of valley, still with these cliffs and mountains on either side. We walk along a colonnade of partial pillars, the roadway paved with hexagonal tiles three feet wide; to the left, steps lead up into The Great Temple, where these pavers stretch maybe 150 feet in, maybe 100 feet across, more of these partial pillars lining its perimeter.

It's starting to get hot out here in the direct sun, no cliff walls to cast shadows. And we still have to get to the Monastery, the base of its trail straight ahead, at the bottom of the mountainside. We've nearly emptied the water bottles we brought with us from the hotel, and though we pass a restaurant nestled up near the mountain, a sunshade tarp and stone place run by the Hilton back in Wadi Musa, we don't stop for more water. We have to get to the Monastery.

Two and a half miles we've walked so far, and now there's the climb up: another mile or so to a height around 700 feet above us. No telling exactly how many steps, but all the guidebooks agree on a ballpark: somewhere between 800 and 1,000. Stone steps, just like the ones that dropped me to a knee. Back where the kids laughed at the tourist.

We start up into the canyon, slowly. Narrow stone steps followed by a trail, stone steps and a trail. Lined on either side at times with open Bedouin tents, inside them souvenirs and souvenirs: necklaces and bracelets and belts and pendants and small boxes all carved from rocks and bones and set with brass and beads. Bright fabrics hang from lines strung between the tents, and the people inside them—mostly women, children too—call out and call out, wanting you to buy.

The cliffs begin to close in on us the higher we get, as though leaning in, alive and looking down on us. This canyon we'd entered is a gorge now, and the trail and steps and trail and steps hug its wall, the gorge growing deeper beside us, the view behind us more stupendous, those reds and mauves and browns all given depth the higher we go, the farther up from them we hike.

Donkeys clatter up and down the steps and trail, each led by a boy holding the reins, and we back up against the walls to let them pass, amazed—no better word—at the audacity of the animals heading up and down with this gorge a couple feet away, but also at the audacity of the tourists riding on them. None looks assured they will live to tell the tale of this trek on a donkey up or down 800 to 1,000 stone steps beside a gorge. But people are riding them, and these donkeys don't seem at all ready to fall.

We take our time. We pause, take photos, walk, pause. We finish our water not a couple hundred steps up, and the May sun shines down. Still the trail climbs and curves, gives views up into wadis that wander into the rock, and façades and tombs here and there, and the ancient and dead city below us: that esplanade, the columns, the plaza all in miniature.

We climb, and climb, and then, as if a miracle, Melanie and I in the midst of all this rock and this heat and this sweating and out-of-breath-altitude—we're over 3,000 feet now—we walk through a narrow pass of stone, one last Bedouin stall to our left, to find before us another plaza of sorts, flat ground fifty yards across, at the far end another a couple of stalls at the base of one last small mountain, a peak finally visible, blue blue sky wide open above us. At our feet is one more set of steps carved into the rock, but this one leads down and to that plaza, and as we move down them, here bursts the Monastery to our right. And finally.

Bigger than the Treasury. A giant façade, maybe 150 feet wide and just as tall carved straight into the red rock. Eight columns in relief on the first level, with a thirty-foot tall doorway ten feet wide into the shallow hall inside the rock. Above that eight more columns with three empty niches between them, on top of all those a broken pediment with a round bowl-like centerpiece, atop that an urn probably fifteen feet high. None of it as intricate as the Treasury, but immense, and imposing, and red rock.

The kind of imposing that makes us stand in this plaza, hands on hips, tired and hot and sweaty and thirsty, but all that forgotten for how big the carved stone façade genuinely is. How beautiful.

We'd read that the purpose of this place, however monumental, is still unknown. Maybe a tomb, maybe a religious gathering place. Two crosses are carved into the rock inside the shallow hall the doorway opens into, so perhaps the place was a Byzantine church.

But standing here, taking it in, the place feels holy for its grandness, its rock, its color and presence. For its being at the top of this city, beneath this blue sky. For its taking the work of climbing so many stairs along such an imposing and beautiful pathway. Its having been carved by the hands of people two thousand years ago, and its still standing here. Here.

People are up here. Old and young. Walking sticks and hats and sunglasses and canteens and backpacks. And those local kids from down on the esplanade, and at the Treasury, and at the mouth of the *siq* and on the trail up here. All up here with donkeys, all calling out for rides back down. The clattering trip down that narrow canyon, and down those uneven and time-worn stone steps.

For a moment we consider this idea, taking donkeys back for how far it is from here to the bottom, and for how hot it is and how late the day is growing. But no. That's crazy. Riding a donkey down. We can walk it when we decide to leave. We can.

We turn from the Monastery to that stall across the plaza. There are tables out front, people lounging there, we can see. It's a kind of restaurant, maybe, with what looks like drinks, perhaps. A bar built into the base of the small peak behind it, and as we get closer, we see there to the left the wide mouth of a cave, and here are rugs on the ground, long rows of low cushions draped with them too, set just inside the cave, and as we enter and our eyes adjust we see more long low cushions and more rugs, the floor of the cave carpeted with them, on them here and there camel saddles to lean against, short and narrow twin-pommeled A-frames with their own rugs. Pushed up against the far wall of the cave, maybe thirty feet back, lies one more long row of cushions to make a kind of low banquette.

It's light in here, the cave mouth high and wide. A few people sit on those cushions, resting, quiet, inside this large cool space, and we see on the ground in front of us pairs of neatly placed hiking sandals and boots. No shoes on the rugs, we understand, and so we take off our hiking sandals, place them neatly in their pairs, and step inside, make our way to the far wall and that banquette.

Then we sit. We lean against the cave wall. We take deep breaths, and look out the cave mouth to where the Monastery stands across that plaza, perfectly framed by the entrance to this timeless and comfortable space.

But we are thirsty. Up to the left and outside the cave is that bar, a kiosk of sorts, and people are in a line out there, and I know, I know, I need to get up from this brief moment of rest to go get us what we need.

Because we need us alive.

I stand, Melanie still leaned against the cool rock wall and smiling because she knows where I'm going and she's too tired to say anything, and I step to the edge of the rugs, slip on my sandals, and go to the queue outside, begin my wait.

But something is up, I can see. The man behind the bar keeps repeating a quick phrase to the couple in front of me until after the third or fourth time I make out the words, "No more bottle water. No more bottle water." He's sweaty too, I can see, and has a moustache and short hair and wears a white long sleeve shirt, and he's working hard to please us all even though there is no bottled water.

And of course I'm regretting whatever stupid voice in me that had said, way back at the base of the climb here when we'd stood beside that restaurant run by the Hilton with its sunshade tarp, that we wouldn't need another bottle of water.

"Only lemon mint water," the man says then, and nods hard at the glass reservoir at the end of the bar to the right I'm only now noticing. Inside is a murky, slightly yellow wash that reaches maybe a third of the way up the two-foot-high glass container. Flecks of green material the size of dimes float around in it, the liquid in there slowly churning: a washing machine mid-cycle.

The couple in front of me, a man and woman dressed very much the same as Melanie and me in our camp shirts and hiking pants, look at each other, then the man, then each other again, then say together, "That's all right, that's all right," and though I'm wanting very much something very cold right then, something in a bottle and clear, I know my options are nil. It will have to be that liquid.

At least it will be cold.

But when I am next, and I tell the man, "Two, please," and after I hand him my five-Dinar note—about eight bucks—and after he sets on the bar two small clear plastic cups of the stuff, then with his fingers plops into each the thinnest thin half-slice of lemon, and after I pick them up, move out of the way of the people behind me and to the mouth of the cave and toward Melanie who looks at this moment like she might very well be asleep, only then do I realize the two cups in my hands are tepid. At best.

Warm, even. Room temperature, I realize.

I smirk. This is the only option here. We will have the whole walk back down that trail and stone steps, that mile through the gorge and to the restaurant where we'll be able to get our bottles of water. This will have to do.

I kick off my sandals, toe them into a neatly placed pair, then go to Melanie, who rouses as I sit beside her, and hand her her cup.

"Lemon mint water," I say. "Room temp," and shake my head. "No water left. Just this."

She smirks too, gives a slow shake of her head, and we hold the cups out, look at that pale yellow murk, these flecks of green. A sad slice of lemon in there, like the white ribcage of some small animal.

And we take our sips.

Of course it's wonderful. Of course it is.

A bright sour aromatic. A quenching. An ache I hadn't known in my throat relieved. No sugar. Just a pucker, cool for the mint.

Just like that. The temperature doesn't even matter, it works so well.

We marvel. We take out our iPhones and each take a picture of our own cup, close up, of this strange little miracle. Perhaps it's our state of mind and body at this moment—worn out by the walk here and over-awed at the view out the mouth of this cave, that massive red rock monument too big even to believe. Maybe.

But this lemon mint water—and this place, this time, this work to get here and what we've received when we have—works.

Yep. We're alive.

We'll walk down. Later. But first, once we're done here, once we've sipped our elixir of wonder, however warm it might be, and once we've rested together, taken deep breaths in and cooled off and maybe closed our eyes for the peace up here, we'll follow a trail to the top of this last little peak behind and above this cave, where we'll take in a view that looks out over all these mountains that have surrounded us all day long. We'll look down crags and gorges and wadis all the way to the Jordan Valley below us, and across to Israel in the far far distance, above it all this blue blue sky. And it will seem we are looking out at the end of the world.

We'll take our pictures of this view, walk down the trail to this plaza and take our pictures of the Monastery, and then we'll start this late afternoon on our way to the bottom of the trail to find that the restaurant with its tarp is closed. No water there. We'll retrace our way back through the esplanade, along those columns, the hexagonal tiles paving the street, and cliffs will begin to close in on us again, lined with those apartments and tombs and memorials. Here will be the amphitheater in the growing shadows, and then the side trail up where I'd fallen to one knee and been exhorted to save my life by a teenage movie star, and then we'll be back to the Treasury, shrouded even deeper by cliff shadow, and then into the *siq*, that long slot canyon with its gutters and striations and still with donkeys and carts we'll choose not to ride, because we're getting close now, close, until we'll make it to the entrance, and head to our hotel, one of a half dozen or so up the desert hill before us.

We'll make it. Because we need ourselves alive. But for now we'll just sip at this lemon mint water, and rest in what feels a very holy moment.

Cherries on the Golan

HOW DO I TELL the story of this day? Because I do not know how to tell it. I don't.

Maybe start here:

We are on the Magical Mystery bus at the end of a long day. Or, the guide, is up front narrating now and again as we drive along a narrow two-lane road. Even inside the bus he wears his thin-brimmed sun hat, hipster hip. Luke, our gang leader and guru and program director, is somewhere in the back of the bus, the rest of us spread around. But I'm not sure if any of us are listening.

We're easing down the western slopes of the Golan Heights, headed a little south and away from Mount Bental, our latest stop. Now we're headed to dinner at a farm restaurant in the Hula Valley, and then we'll head back to the hotel in Nazareth.

Orchards beside us. The setting sun to our right flickers into the bus from between the rows of cherry trees over there. Cherry trees on our left too, this two-lane lined with them, and I am reminded of being a kid in Southern California, way back in the 1960s, when Orange County was a place where they grew things, and the roads were lined with strawberry and tomato fields, and groves of orange and plum and peach trees. Orchards just like these, and light just like this, as my dad drives the green '56 Dodge pickup he inherited when his father died in 1965, we three brothers in the bed and watching the rows go by. Mom and Dad and our little sister are up in the cab, all of us headed home from somewhere: the beach, or a picnic in Irvine, or at the end of an evening drive.

Mount Bental. A hill among a low line of hills, Mount Hermon to the left and rising above everything. A beautiful vista point at the top end of the country, the place a kind of park to take in these views. But a park set in remembrance of the place where 177 Israeli tanks held off 1,500 Syrian tanks during the Yom Kippur War in 1973. A hilltop riven with old bunkers and bulwarked trenches that sits above and beside the present Syrian border. There was a touristy restaurant up there, on the menu *café hafuch*, *burekas*, and Israeli salad. Cheese sandwiches and tuna salad. Pizza. Patrons sat outside on the wooden deck and looked out onto Syria, Damascus only thirty-six miles in the distance.

Life-size iron silhouettes of soldiers were scattered across the grounds looking down onto Syria. Some knelt with rifles aimed, others held binoculars up to survey the land, another climbing up out of a trench, rifle slung over his shoulder, headed into action. Children in the cool afternoon wind played hide and seek in those bunkers and trenches while we were there, the border fence visible right down the hill maybe a mile or so away, just down there.

Between that hilltop outpost and the fence lay farmland, green and alive, rows and rows of green, while just the other side of the fence the land turned dry, desolate. What looked like the destroyed foundations of a town sat a little farther off, empty streets and flat concrete squares where houses once stood.

Syria, where, as we'd stood and looked out over this all, the country was in the midst of a war against itself.

A strange and peaceful hilltop of celebration and mourning at once. The low saddle to the left between Mount Bental and the next hilltop, Mount Hermonit three and a half miles to the north, was named the Valley of Tears on only the second day of the four-day battle in 1973, so many burning tanks littered there. Of the 100 or so Israeli tanks engaged in the valley, only twenty or thirty were left by the end. Yet the Israelis held the line: of the 500 Syrian tanks engaged, 300 were destroyed before they retreated. The enemy was routed.

We'd all walked those trenches, stood looking out at this country at war right then, right there. We'd looked out on the flat valley where so many died a couple wars before this one. We looked out onto the border fence between these two countries, and the land either side of it. Green, and dry.

The fence. A place about which we'd been told a story earlier on this long day. A good story. One we were remembering as we stood there, and looked down on this other country.

Or maybe start here:

We are on the bus, early morning. We're staying in Nazareth, at the Golden Crown Hotel, and had found yet again a buffet breakfast beyond belief waiting for us in the hotel restaurant. Twenty yards of fruit, vegetables, salads, cheeses, hummus and bagels and *burekas* and breads and eggs—scrambled, hard-boiled—and juices squeezed on the spot, and of course *hafuch*, and cappuccini and plain old American coffee.

This will be the longest day yet: tonight we'll end with dinner at a farmhouse restaurant in the Hula Valley, the agricultural flatland above the Sea of Galilee, but along the way we'll have a talk and lunch with a man who is translating the Bible into Aramaic, and there'll be a stop at a place on the Golan Heights called Mount Bental. But we're starting with a visit to a hospital in Tsvat—Safed—and a doctor there who will tell us a story. All of it in the far north end of the country.

We pile onto the bus, happy, laughing, full already after that breakfast, then head through the already-snarl of traffic downtown Nazareth always is, and head back up north, through Cana and that side street we'd headed away on to find Sindyanna of Galilee and the story of women and olive oil and purpose. Now we're headed to another place and, on this magical tour, another story, and it occurs to me as we head out of town, the city falling away to reveal the dry dusty hills around us, that we are story-gathering this whole trip.

We're being given stories, one after another. Because stories are what matters. Stories are who we are. Stories are how we build our lives, and how we build our communities, and how we build love.

Stories are how we live.

Maybe back to here:

Still the sunset in through the windows of the bus—that sputtering light through the groves—splashes in on us. The day is growing cooler, though once we get to the farm restaurant we'll swelter at our table inside. But on Mount Bental the wind up from the Syrian side had made us hunch a bit, hands in pockets, though it was June. Shadows of summer clouds overhead—some gray and laden enough to threaten rain—dappled the landscape below, the hilltop itself in shadow.

But the sunlight was now certain, if only broken by these groves. And now tall, thin Or stands up at the front of the bus, and leans forward a bit toward the driver, his eyes ahead of us and that narrow two-lane road, his head moving back and forth, looking for something out there.

Then he turns to us, says, "Who would like cherries?"

Or start with this place:

Before Mount Bental, on the long road up from the Hula Valley, and after a lunch of endless salads at Shadi Khalloul's home in Jish just beside the Lebanon border, we'd stopped for a moment and taken pictures of Nimrod's Fortress a mile to the north, on the slopes up the side of Mount Hermon. A ragged line of stone walls with vestiges of a turret now and again a few hundred yards long: a far-off row of broken teeth upon a mountainside. Saladin's nephew built it there in 1228—atop Byzantine ruins—to protect against Crusader invasions of Damascus through the low saddle of land to its left, the valley there between smaller Mount Hermonit and Mount Bental on the Golan Heights. Syria sits just past them, though we can't yet see it from here.

That saddle is where the Mongols, invading from Damascus in 1260, broke through, captured, then dismantled the fortress we all looked upon right then.

Or sketched out the story for us as we'd climbed down from the bus at a pullout so we could take our pictures, and there seemed some childlike mystery in what we beheld, some storybook echo from within these tales of yore: Saladin, Crusaders, Kublai Khan invading from afar.

But there was war inside the story too. Of course there was war.

Where were we, but the Middle East?

And we'd been told a story earlier, at the hospital. A good one, but one about war all the same.

Maybe start here, because it too is part of the story. And because I don't yet know how to tell the story at the hospital:

We'd driven north and west out of Tsvat and the hospital, through hill country and hill country, on our way to the next stop, a place called Baram National Park. The bus lumbered off the main road onto another two-lane, beside us pine and cedar, then slowed into a gravel lot, where we dutifully climbed out.

In the lot stood a man in his forties wearing a white short-sleeve camp shirt and black pants. Black hair, tan, smiling: a handsome and happy dude. Luke was first to him, handshakes and hugs, then Luke introduced him to Or, and then to us all.

Shadi Khalloul, who lived just down the road in Jish, and who was translating the entire Bible into Aramaic, the original language Christ used. The whole Bible.

But for now we were here to see the ancient synagogue, and the old Maronite church.

The park sat at the top of a hill amidst those same trees, and we walked along a road through them first to Kfar Baram Synagogue, built in the third and fourth century and destroyed in an epic earthquake mid-nineteenth century, the remains of it all leached in the gray and black pall of time and weather. Ruins now, except for the first-floor façade and the low ring of exterior walls, the floors inside and three aisles where pillars had at one time stood. Still, the ruins allowed a sense of the former grandeur of the place: in front of the façade stood evidence of six columns to what had been a portico, the façade itself with three doorways facing Jerusalem, all basalt stone. Above the center doorway was an archway carved with reliefs of grape clusters and leaves, curved dentil molding and crown molding too. Carved into the stone above the door on the right, Shadi made certain to point out, was the name of the builder, written in Aramaic. An elongated scramble of shapes barely visible, but a name in an ancient language. There in stone.

Then we walked along another gravel road and to the Maronite church, built post-earthquake. A small and modest stone chapel with a belltower topped with a thin iron cross. An almost Moorish curved archway hung over the doorway into the chapel, the lintel above carved with images of its own: what seemed perhaps two lambs, four overlapping Templar-looking crosses, four round protrusions with crossing lines on each. All so very much more primitive than the elegant synagogue reliefs above the doorway there. All of it humble.

A Maronite village had existed here for centuries, Shadi told us once we were inside and seated for a talk on his work translating the Bible. Lebanese Christians, the Maronites thrived in their own way through centuries of domination and persecution, their faith traced back to the fourth century and St. Maron's apostle, Abraham of Cyrrhus. A Syrian hermit, Abraham realized the Phoenicians had not yet been evangelized, and left home to bring them Christ. This chapel was still used for celebrations and observances.

Then onto the bus and a drive down from the hilltop to a town called Jish, the bus driver maneuvering us along narrow stone street after street after alley after alley just as smoothly as when we'd headed to Sindyanna. We clapped for him when finally we pulled up to a plaza of sorts and he parked under an olive tree, the bus leaning to the left a good ten degrees for the slope of the plaza, and then we climbed out, took in the view up the hill from here, the tiers of homes layered along this hillside.

Across from us lay rocky hill country dotted with trees, below us a steep valley a couple hundred feet deep, on the hillsides dirt roads and some tracts of green farmland, the horizon perhaps a couple miles away.

We followed Shadi across the small plaza to a stone house whose doorway was hung with a curtain of beads to keep out the bugs and to let in whatever cool air could be found on the breezes up this high. This was his house, and he welcomed us in and to the front room just inside. A long and narrow room set with three folding tables of differing lengths and widths end to end, paper tablecloths on them, mismatched wooden chairs all around. The tables were set for all seventeen of us and Shadi too with plates and forks and knives and glasses and colorful paper napkins, and then suddenly a number of smiling and nodding women in kerchiefs and long skirts began moving in and out between this room and what had to be the kitchen to the left, all of it in a kind of choreographed service, a welcoming liturgy of food, each bringing out a bowl or dish or plate of what would be the most generous and humble and refreshing and *tasty* lunch of the entire trip.

Salads.

Here were bowls of Israeli salad, of course, bright red and deep green and white for their peppers and tomatoes and cucumbers and onions, but sprinkled with feta on top and croutons—cubed and baked challah, we would find out—and flat leaf parsley atop it too. There were dishes of hummus pooled at their centers with olive oil and whole chickpeas, and plates of roasted eggplant and tomato salad, kernels of corn in there too, these salads glistening with soft shards of purple and red and yellow and more of that white white feta. Bowls of white *labneh* flecked with green herbs and artfully puddled just as the hummus with olive oil. Mixed salads of romaine and tomato for the less adventurous palates among us, and a rough-cut kind of slaw of cabbage and carrots and more parsley, plates stacked with pitas cut in two, tall bottles of cold water, pitchers of orange juice and tea.

And all these women coming in and going out of the kitchen still delivered it all, all of them smiling and nodding in their kerchiefs and long skirts.

We were welcomed, and we ate, and we cheered the women when at the end Luke called for them to come from the kitchen, where they had eaten while Shadi spoke of his work with the Aramaic, and why it was important to have the entire Bible in the vernacular of Christ as He spoke when He was among us.

Because He was God among us. And because He spoke to us in this language.

We listened, and prayed, and thanked Shadi for the ongoing story of his work.

And cheered for the food, and the women who gave it to us.

Just before getting back on the bus, we stood on the plaza looking out across the rocky valley and the farmland over there, the thin network of dirt roads.

One of us asked how far Lebanon was from here, and Shadi answered, "That is Lebanon right over there." He pointed to the horizon. "We are nearly on the border right here," and we all stood in wonder, looking to this foreign country known for its wars with Israel, and its wars with itself, and its wars with Syria. Lebanon, just over there.

Later, back on the bus and down the hill through those alleys and streets, we were riding along a highway headed north toward the next stop—a place called Mount Bental on the Golan Heights—when there arose among us a kind of quiet clamor, low talk and puzzlement. One and then another and then all of us noticed our phones had each received a new text message.

Welcome to Lebanon! we read, and the accompanying info on texts and phone calls our telephone companies gave when entering a new country.

We all held up our phones to show each other, and Or, up front, stood and turned to us, said, "This is the border," and nodded to his right.

Directly out the window, just across the oncoming lane, stood a wire fence eight feet tall, beyond it a gravel road precisely paralleling the one we drove. On the other side of that road and a few feet up the hillside lay a double row of concertina wire, one atop another.

"That's Lebanon," Or called out.

Maybe back to this:

"We will stop for cherries," Or calls out, decision made just like that without assent or otherwise from anyone on the bus, and he stoops to the driver, says something to him, Or's head moving back and forth, still scanning for something out there.

Then he says something quick, sharp, and points ahead and to his left, and the bus driver pulls over to the right and onto the shoulder, these groves beside us even closer now, the sun even lower through them. The shards of light slow down among us, until their movement stops altogether, and we are all bathed in pieces of light in through the windows.

But here is the story. The one I do not know how to tell, and for that reason have buried it here near the end, because I don't know how to tell this so that it works. So that it will be right.

So that these words will have the meaning they need to give what the story already owns, outright and all on its own, no help from me and these words piled up. The story I do not know how to tell, and which I am afraid in my telling will diminish its meaning, its worth.

Here:

The road to the hospital in Tsvat—Ziv Medical Center—climbs north and west from Nazareth up a four-lane highway, the hillside out our window to the left sloping down gently, then not so gently, until we are high up on the side of the hill, pines across the low hills we look out at. This will be our first stop on the longest day yet of the trip, bright morning sunlight illuminating the land all around us, and slowly, slowly, buildings appear to our right, first low-lying, then two story, and three, and four. All apartments, square buildings the color of sand.

It's a city we are nearing, this four-lane on the edge of it, one side these hills, the other these buildings, and then the bus reels through a roundabout, and now we are headed up at an even sharper angle, these buildings on both sides of us now.

Tsvat. Safed. The highest city in all Israel, we have been told, at 3,000 feet. An ancient city founded some time in the bronze age, possibly—legend has it—by one of Noah's sons. A city fought over century through century, won and lost by Crusaders, Saladin, Crusaders, the Malmuks, the Ottomans, the British, the Arabs and, now, the Israelis. One of the five cities in ancient Israel where fires were lit to signal to surrounding lands the start of God-ordained festivals and observances.

Modern now: apartment buildings, roundabouts, traffic, and then the bus eases to the right and onto a spur from that highway up, and slowly we make our way toward a very modern complex: five stories, each floor a row of flat stone topped with a recessed balcony. A broad stone plaza out front, to the right the emergency entrance with its portico for ambulances. Past that and perpendicular to the main building another, lower wing with its stone floors and balconies. A manicured lawn inside the ambulance roundabout, grass edged with bright red and white flowers.

A hospital. Perched atop a hill.

Inside, we are welcomed by an older man in a blue short-sleeve dress shirt and dark slacks, gray-haired and with glasses. He's quiet and purposeful as he shakes each of our hands one by one, smiling, nodding. He's the director here, a doctor—of course—and leads us through first a bright reception area and then down hallway and hallway until we are ushered into a lecture room, rows of seats in tiers, each with a fold down desktop, all facing a white screen on the wall. A projector hangs from the ceiling and is already on, a map of Israel on that screen but pale for the fact the lights are still on.

We take our seats—there are maybe fifty in the room, we seventeen spread out as though we are aloof undergrads the first day of class—and the director welcomes us, thanks us for being here, then asks Luke to turn off the lights.

He shows us slide after slide of maps, and numbers, and graphs, all while telling us about the medical center, the region, the vast area Ziv serves: all of the Upper Galilee and northern Golan Heights. Two hundred fifty thousand residents up here, urban and rural alike. Muslims and Jews and Christians and Druze, his medical staff likewise made up of people from these same groups. Its mission of healing.

Then a story.

The man in the blue short-sleeve dress shirt, this doctor, tells us of a night in February 2013. The civil war next door—Syrian rebels against the government of Bashar al-Assad—was in its second year. Already perhaps 70,000 dead. Though Israel had had no incursions, the war was active just beyond the border fences on the north and east side of the country. Israeli Defense Forces had installed triage stations along the border in case the war ruptured into the country.

And one night a routine patrol along the border—two young soldiers in a vehicle—came to a point on the fence where they found seven Syrian soldiers lying just outside the wire. All of them wounded, all of them critically.

This up on the Golan Heights, the fence up there.

The soldiers called in what they'd found to the nearest triage station. What do we do? they asked.

Moments passed with no answer.

Then: Bring them in, as many as you can. We will send another vehicle for those you can't fit.

But once at the triage station, the medics there assess they cannot be of the help these seven need. They're just a triage station. They are only IDF medics.

What do we do? they asked.

They called Ziv Medical Center, warned them they were bringing in seven Syrian soldiers who had been left at the border.

Then I say it.

I am too loud. I am not thinking about the others, or any kind of protocol. Of waiting for the Q and A to come, or interrupting the whole presentation.

I say it, and loud, because they are the words that come to me in that moment. Too loud.

But I say it just the same:

"Even your enemies know you are good."

The doctor pauses, looks at me from the lectern. He does not nod, or smile. He does nothing other than look at me, the room quiet a moment, a moment. Then he continues with the story.

From then on Syrian soldiers began trickling in to the hospital, left at the border—at that wire—one, and another, and more.

Then Syrian citizens began to appear in the night, injured—a girl and her mother with shrapnel wounds, a boy nearly dead from a bomb explosion—and seeking to be taken care of by Israelis.

So far, on this day we are visiting, 470 Syrians have been treated. All but five survived and have been returned to their country.

Over 5,000 Syrians are eventually treated in hospitals across the country.

And eighteen Syrian babies have been born here, at Ziv.

Even their enemies know they are good.

Or hops down from the bus and crosses the two-lane bordered by these cherry groves, and we watch out our windows him at the makeshift cherry stand there on the shoulder across from us. Cartons of cherries cover the top of the table there, and Or talks to a woman in a long skirt and kerchief, and she nods, hands him two cartons of cherries, and Or hands her some money, and they both nod, smile at each other.

A moment later Or is back on the bus. "Cherries!" he says, and holds them up, then hands a carton to one side of the bus, one to the other, and they begin their ways down the rows, we travelers partaking, and suddenly in my hand and in Melanie's are glistening, deep red cherries. Three or four each.

They are beautiful.

Once the lecture is over, Luke turns the lights back on and we ask our questions and receive our answers (Do any of them choose to stay? No. Are any of them angry they are here? Some, yes. Were those first soldiers rebels or Bashar al-Assad's? To which, for this question, the doctor answers with a question of his own: Why do you ask?, then tells us it does not matter, because they are in need.), and then we are ushered out of the room and back into the hallway and into another until we are now in the adjoining wing, the one perpendicular to the main wing and which we'd seen outside when we pulled up.

The children's wing, he tells us.

We can take no pictures, the doctor in the short-sleeve blue shirt tells us. He can give us no names of who we will see. This is because they are Syrian, here from the border. They have come to seek help, as others before them have.

A child, six or seven years old, and the child's mother. The child has a malady we are not allowed to record, because when the child is healed, they will return to their home, and as with all who have been here and treated, they do not want those in Syria to know they have been to the enemy's hospital. Because there have been cases of retribution. Families have been murdered at news such as this.

Then we are in a hospital room. A small child seems swamped within white blankets and sheets there in the bed, a machine attached and beeping. But the child is awake, and smiles at us while the doctor speaks to the child words in Arabic. Beside the child, in a chair pushed as flush to the bed as it can be, sits the mother, a younger woman in a long skirt and blouse with a shawl around her and wearing a kerchief. She barely looks at us, her eyes to her hands in her lap, glancing up only now and again at the doctor, then back to her hands.

It is a strange moment, we visitors inside a room so small we move in and out in self-appointed shifts for the few minutes we are there. We are strangers, and it seems we have no business here other than to see this child, and this mother. To see the good being done, though I already know and believe in the good here.

After a few minutes of the doctor speaking to the child, the mother, and to us—how long the child has been here, how long before heading home, how bewildering it is for the child, how stressful for the mother—we are leaving the room.

But not before the mother looks up at us all, and smiles, and nods, and says with this gesture, *Thank you.* Though we have nothing about which we are to be thanked. We are merely witnesses.

We are those receiving her story, and her child's story, and the story of this hospital, and its work.

Once out in the hallway, Luke calls out that it's time to go, and apologizes to the doctor for the fact we have a long day ahead of us, and thanks him too, and I find myself at the rear of the pack as we move down the hallway to another and then toward the bright reception area where we first entered.

Here is the doctor beside me as we walk. The older man in the blue short-sleeve dress shirt, graying hair and glasses, who has brought us all this.

And I speak again. But this time I am quieter. Because I am going to ask a question about me. Because I want to know who I am in this.

Maybe I am being selfish. But it is the question that comes to me in the light of and in the wake of and in the display and revelation and *vista* of this story.

"What can I do?" I ask him, quietly.

The doctor stops then and I do too, the rest of us all moving down the hallway and toward a bus that sits in a hilltop hospital parking lot, waiting to take us to all that lay ahead of us this day.

He looks at me, his eyes right on mine.

"Tell this story," he says.

And I say, "I will." I say, "I will." Because even as he says the words, I am already trying to figure out a way to tell this story. How I can make it seem real. How I can do what I have been asked to do, and want to do, and know I have to do.

But I don't know how.

I don't even know how to do this.

But I'm trying. Right now, here.

There are these cherries in our hands. Deep red, green stems. We are in the Golan Heights.

The bus starts up again, eases out onto the two-lane, and shuddering light through the groves begins again to shine upon us all.

Ahead of us lies a farmhouse restaurant where we will swelter during our dinner. Then a drive back to Nazareth, where we will be delivered late this evening, and we will troop to our beds and fall asleep and dream our dreams.

Behind us, behind us: story and story and story.

But now: This is when I pick a cherry from my hand and pop it into my mouth. The stem is between my lips, and I twist it off, then bite down on the fruit, careful about the pit, that miserable unwelcome predictable surprise every time.

But the flavor: a small exuberant burst upon the tongue, bright and sweet and deep and carrying with it all of time, the richness of this earth, the peace it offers, the bounty, the goodness.

Splintered light through groves. A smile.

A cherry.

Oh the hollowness of my words. The emptiness of them, the disheveled string of them all I can muster to describe this story of a cherry on the Golan: bright, sweet, fresh. Alive. Full.

There is a child in a bed in a hospital very far from home.

This is the story, the surprise at the end of a very long day:

God is good.

Sabbath

OUR APARTMENT IN German Colony was only a ten-minute walk to the gardens that overlooked the old city. To the left stood the high limestone walls of Jerusalem, to the right Mt. Zion itself with its trees and tiers of white buildings, the blue cone roof of Dormition Abbey, beside it the white belltower. In the evenings all that fall we lived there Melanie and I took walks to the gardens, the limestone walkways lined with rosemary, olive trees everywhere. And this view of Jerusalem.

We live here, we said to each other. That's Jerusalem. That's it. Right there.

But we also *lived* there. We went to the grocers, the post office, the ATM. The gas station, the butcher shop, the laundromat. I made my routine drives down to Tel Aviv to teach my courses and attend meetings. All that.

We *lived* there.

Which meant dealing with Shabbat. That pesky Saturday when nothing—or very little—was open. No news in how we Americans felt: Even though we are believing Christians, we still found it difficult to adjust. Of course we were used to going where we needed to go and doing what we needed to do. Yes, we understood the holiness of the day, God's call to observe the Sabbath one of those really real commandments.

Still, those first few weeks we were sometimes a little piqued about the whole thing. Especially if we'd missed going to the grocer's, or the butcher's, or just wanted an Everything with Bulgarian cream cheese from Tal Bagel down the street.

But one Saturday early on we decided to take a mid-morning walk to the gardens, because there wasn't a whole lot to do. And the bagel place was closed.

Here was the rosemary, the olive trees. The limestone walls of the city, that blue cone roof and belltower.

But there were also people out walking. A lot of them. Young people, old. Families. Couples. Many were Orthodox of one kind or another, the men with their hats, the women with their long skirts and scarves. Boys with their kippahs, girls in pretty dresses.

Then the dim bulb of understanding came to us, the unsurprising no-news of what a Sabbath really is. The life-long call finally, finally made manifest to the weak-eyed and hard of hearing.

This is a day *off.*

This is a day of *rest.*

And the commandment in full seemed to fall into place: I have created you in My image, and I want you to enjoy one day of rest a week, because I know the joy of that peaceful day. This rest I offer you is so important it is in fact holy. So take this day off to rest in My Name.

Nothing new. At all. But a discovery we two made one Saturday morning in Jerusalem.

"Shabbat Shalom," these people out walking in the gardens called to each other, and to us. Peace to you this Sabbath.

"Shabbat Shalom," we said in return, and began to understand.

Acknowledgments

THIS BOOK IS a strange one. It comes out of a desire not to let pass away places we've been and people we've met and food we've eaten through all these years. It also comes out of thankfulness for the ways we have been blessed. Because we have been blessed. Beyond measure.

Those blessings have to include, for starters, Michael Richards who, as first a friend and fellow writer all those years ago in Massachusetts, would end up being the one who would invite us to Israel in the first place. None of this could have happened without his asking us to come, and to help.

Of course I count all the people with the U. S. State Department who worked to bring us there time and again, and who saw us through our adventures while there. They know who they are, and I am thankful for them.

A genuine blessing was the creative writing faculty at Bar-Ilan University, who were good and faithful colleagues while we lived there and on our return trips, Allen Hoffman and Michael Kramer especially.

And I am thankful for the blessing of Shaindy Rudolf, and her having asked me at the cocktail party so long ago if I would even consider living in Israel and teaching there. She remains a blessing to this day to all students who study writing at Bar-Ilan.

Whether they know it or not, that gang of student writers in my workshop at Bar-Ilan was a grand blessing too, patient with the new guy in town as I made my way through living in that foreign land. I looked forward to meeting with them every week, to reading their work, to talking with them about their lives, and to listening.

Linda and Donald Zisquit, as testified to in the prior pages, were and remain dear friends, and were integral to our experiences in Jerusalem, and I am thankful for having them in our lives. Donald: I look forward to our next conversation.

And there's another whole flight of people who have been blessings to us, beginning with Luke Moon of the Philos Project, and the immense generosity that program exhibited to us and the participants in our enlightening trip on the bus. They are: Mike Cosper, Mako Fujimura, Gina Oschner, Sandra McCracken, Eric Lige, Michael and Shanaka Winters, Dave and Amanda Harrity, and Lachlan Coffey. And where would we have been without Or Rein, our illustrious guide in that hipster hat?

Angela and Jess Correll have been blessings not only to Melanie and me for many years now, but also to more people than any of us can ever know. Their generosity and hospitality know no bounds, and we are thankful we can call them friends.

A blessing that has extended through our lives for going-on four decades now has been Jeff and Hart Deal. Not only did they visit us while we lived in Israel, but also while we lived in Annot, France, and while we were spending a summer month each year in Umbria, Italy. Oh, and there was that twenty-six-day road trip in the RV across eleven states too. The amazing blessing: we're still friends.

Greg Wolfe has been a blessing for decades now too, and I am thankful for his friendship and his editorial acumen. This book would not be here without him.

Marian Young, my agent since 1985, has been a blessing throughout, and my small note here to thank her for taking such good care of me as a writer for all these years does not do justice to how much I appreciate her.

Finally, but always, I have been blessed by Melanie, my wife, in ways that can only be due to the generosity of our God and Creator. Since she read the first story of mine when I was an RC Cola salesman taking a creative writing class at the local community college, Melanie promptly dismissing it with a rueful smile and shake of her head as being pretty lousy (which it was), I have known I love her, and have been blessed by her honesty, patience, intelligence and grace for more than forty years now. God bless you, Melanie, and thank you.

Soli Deo gloria!

ACKNOWLEDGMENTS

The author would like to thank the editors of the following journals in which these essays originally appeared:

"Sabbath" in *Brevity*
"Security" in *River Teeth*
"On *Za'atar*" in *Creative Nonfiction*
"Olives in Jerusalem" in *Talking River Review*

Some names have been changed.

This book was set in Minion Pro, a typeface created by the renowned designer, Robert Slimbach, and inspired by late-Renaissance typefaces in the humanist style.

This book was designed by Shannon Carter, Ian Creeger, and Gregory Wolfe. It was published in hardcover, paperback, and electronic formats by Slant Books, Seattle, Washington.

Cover art: *Mount of Olives, Jerusalem*, 1876; Lockwood de Forest, brush and oil paint, graphite on paper board.